The Great Argo Project:

The Tunnel, Mill, and Millionaire

By
Terry Cox

TCox & Associates, LLC
Golden, Colorado

> The wrap-around photograph used for the front and back covers shows the mill essentially intact. Only a few windows had been broken and the painted names of the mill and tunnel had not faded substantially. It seems probable that the photo dates from the early 1950s. EPA's water treatment facility is now situated near where the tall tipple once stood—
> *Historical Society of Idaho Springs.*

The Great Argo Project: The Tunnel, Mill, and Millionaire
by Terry Cox

© 2022 by Terry Cox

All rights reserved. No part of this book may be reproduced without written permission from the publisher, with the exception of short passages for review purposes.

Books may be purchased in quantity by contacting the publisher by email at tcox@coxrail.com.

Published by TCox & Associates, LLC, Golden, Colorado.

Library of Congress Control Number: 2022948628

ISBN-13: 978-0-9746485-2-1

Printed in the United States of America.
First edition.
Printed: 2022

ACKNOWLEDGMENTS

One can only imagine the thousands of times we passed the Argo Mill during the thirteen years Lynda and I lived in Idaho Springs. More than a few times, we discussed that *someone* needed to tell it's story, as well as the story of the Argo Tunnel sitting to its left. It wasn't until much later that pressure to undertake the project developed.

The pressurizing squad consisted of Mary Jane Loevlie (the ring-leader), Janice Bowland and my lovely wife Lynda (the tag team) and Robert Bowland (the cheer leader). It seems that none of the four actually listened to any of my protests about "other things I need to do."

Everyone knows that books like this are never written alone. I was fortunate to have the help of Janice Bowland, Robert Bowland, Allii Curran, Dustin Littleton, and Lynda Cox. All read the text, pointed out errors, and kept me focused on telling the story in language as non-technical as possible. We are collectively in debt to Don Allan who scanned most of the photographs in the collection of the Historical Society of Idaho Springs. Equally important is Dan Keller who took over from Don and generously compiled Argo images from that collection for me to choose from. Finally, I applaud everyone involved in The Mighty Argo Gold Mill & Tunnel project for working to preserve this important monument to Colorado history.

I sincerely thank all of you.

GLOSSARY OF MINING TERMS

ADIT. A horizontal passage leading into a mine.

AMALGAMATION. The process by which mercury is alloyed with gold, silver, copper or other metals. If you've ever stuck mercury to a ring or a silver or copper coin, you've seen amalgamation in action.

CLAIM. A parcel of public land that a person is legally entitled to mine.

LODE. A valuable mineral deposit found in the earth's surface; generally synonymous with vein or lead.

MILL. An industrial plant used to recover valuable metals and concentrate ore into smaller volumes.

ORE. The commercially profitable portion of a mineral deposit; most gold and silver ores in the vicinity were sulfur minerals that also contained significant quantities of copper, lead, and zinc.

PAN. A circular pan used for finding gold, generally 10 to 16 inches in diameter and 2 to 3 inches deep, with sloping sides and made out of steel, copper, or plastic; also used as a verb to prospect for placers.

PLACER. A sand and gravel deposit that contains valuable quantities of gold and silver. (Pronounced like "plaster" without the "t.")

PORTAL. Horizontal entrance to a mine or tunnel, normally designed to protect the opening from collapse.

RAISE. A shaft driven *upwards* from a mine level or access tunnel.

SHAFT. A vertical, or nearly vertical, hole dug *downward* in the ground, analogous to an elevator shaft. Shafts may extend from the surface downward or between different levels of a mine. Most shafts in the vicinity were dug along veins and were inclined as much as twenty degrees from vertical with some tilted significantly more.

SLUICE. A long, trough-like box through which placer gravel is washed by a stream of water; gold particles are caught in the bottom by rocks, wooden bars, metal bars, cloth, or carpet.

SMELT. To separate valuable metals from worthless rock by melting ore in a furnace.

STOPE. To mine much or all vein material from between valueless wall rock; also used as a noun to describe the empty void left after "stoping." (Pronounced with a long "o.")

VEIN. A clearly-defined zone of mineralized rock generally having a somewhat regular development in length, width, and depth.

CONTENTS

Glossary of Mining Terms 4
Introduction 7
Argo Tunnel 9
Argo Mill 53
Samuel Newhouse 85
Timeline of Mining-Related Events 115
References 117
Endnotes 123
Index 125

MAPS

Area Covered in This Book 6
Argo Tunnel and Nearby Mines 25
Profile of the Argo Tunnel 32-33
Argo Tunnel, Laterals and Connected Mines 34
Argo Tunnel Progress, 1893-1910 39
Mines Known to Have Processed Ore at the Argo Mill 64-65
Idaho Springs and Mills in Competition with the Argo Mill 78-79
Manhattan Land Play by Samuel & Mott Newhouse 99

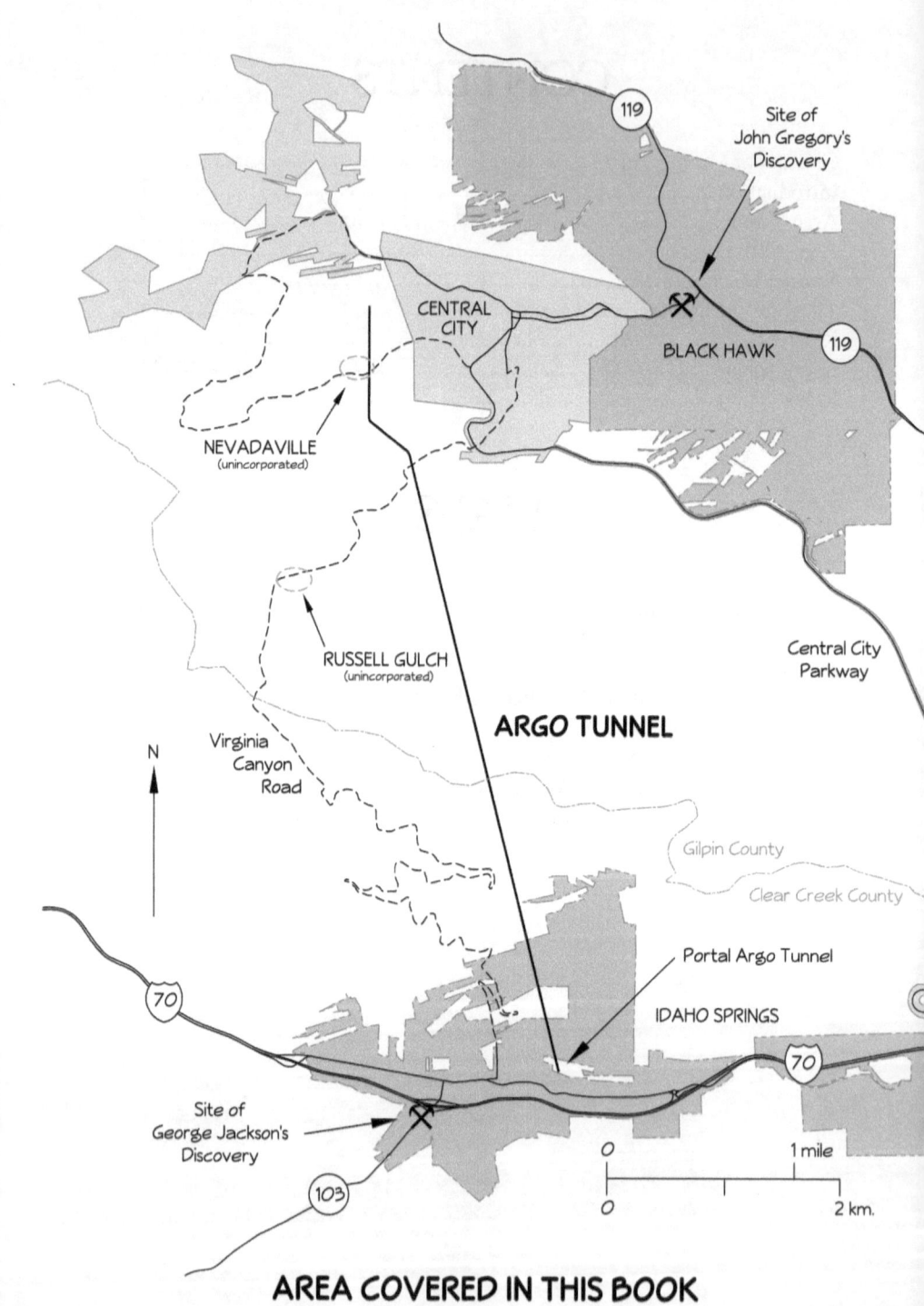

AREA COVERED IN THIS BOOK

INTRODUCTION

I suspect most people who thumb through this book will be visiting one of many Colorado towns founded on mining. Some of those places are now synonymous with entertainment and visitors may not realize those towns' earlier dependencies on gold and silver mining. Fortunately, a few proudly display their histories of mining and mineral wealth through both their old buildings and their surrounding mountainsides.

Mining is not as old as the hills, of course, but it is as ancient as the oldest civilizations. Although modernized, some of the oldest techniques of extraction and processing are still used in today's gold mining. Some of mining's very oldest challenges also remain.

Although I will discuss mining in this book to some extent, that is not my goal. In truth, the concept of mining is really quite simple. Identify the commodity needed, find the rocks that hold it, dig those rocks out of the ground, and process them.

Yes, every step can be tremendously challenging, but the idea itself is not.

Gold and silver are called "precious metals." One of the best things about the precious metals business is that there is a ready market for every ounce of metal pulled from the ground. The market, however, is utterly agnostic. The market does not care whether an ounce of gold came from a tiny mine in Colorado or a huge mine on the other side of the world. After it is refined, gold is gold.

It is true that adjacent mines compete against each other over labor, transportation, and supplies. In actuality, every gold and silver mine in the world competes against every other, not merely the mine next door. Mines compete solely on the basis of cost—how much it costs to extract an ounce of metal. Every mine has is own unique problems to solve, and their individual costs of mining reflect how well they do that. No mine, not even government-run operations, can stay in business for long if it costs more to mine gold than the market is willing to pay.

The Argo Tunnel and Argo Mill served an area on the border between Gilpin and Clear Creek Counties, an area that surrounds the first two gold discoveries every made in the mountains of Colorado. Every operation within that area faced two problems that outweighed all others: the difficulty of separating gold and silver from rock and the high costs of removing excess water from mines.

Realistically, very few gold mines on the planet have ever escaped either problem, let alone both. Ironically, it is that very commonality, the global presence of water and the challenges of separating gold from rock, that levels the industry. Those two problems are ubiquitous and cause so much anguish and expense that they actually allow *all* mines, just the giant ones, to compete on a global scale.

A relatively small area in Gilpin County, about 20 square miles, was the state's greatest gold producer for many years after discovery, but its output had hit its high point in 1871. By 1890, it had become dramatically apparent that flooding was causing more and more miners to abandon the deepest parts of their mines and, ultimately, to walk away from their mines entirely. Samuel Newhouse saw the problem, realized that a large drainage tunnel would benefit the district, and believed that mines would readily pay to solve their worsening water problems. This book tells the story that resulted from his decision to drain that fabulous gold district by digging a 4.2-mile (6.7 km) tunnel under the mountains.

His initial idea included the building of a mill near the tunnel in order to process the massive quantities of ore he hoped would emerge from its portal. That mill was finally built after the tunnel reached its ultimate length in 1910.

I want to stress to readers that the Argo Tunnel was a long hole in the ground, to be sure. But, it was NOT a mine. It was designed as a way to *access* numerous mines. Its goal was to make money by hauling ore and draining mines along its length.

Samuel Newhouse had been involved with mining for twelve years before he ever put miners to work on the Argo Tunnel and he stayed involved with mining for practically the rest of his life. His life was every bit as interesting as the Argo Tunnel and his other projects, so I spend the last third of this book talking about him.

I hope readers will forgive me for violating two norms of books of this size.

First, I added a glossary in the *front* of the book instead of politely hiding it in the back.

Second, I added endnotes to the back of the book to allow curious readers to check the sources I consulted. That is rarely done in a book of this size and intent.

The gold mining business is one heavily decorated with terrific stories. In general, most of those stories are true–*to a point*. It is important to remember , however, that humans often prefer exaggeration and liberal interpretation to mere facts. While mysteries abound, there are a good many stories and printed "facts" about the Argo Tunnel, the Argo Mill, and Samuel and Ida Newhouse. I hate saying it, but some do not stand up well to scrutiny. For that reason, I refrained from mentioning several fascinating "facts" rather than deflating oft-told, compelling, and fanciful tales. Instead, I chose to give readers a way to check *my* so-called facts.

Finally, I feel the story of Samuel and Ida Stingley Newhouse deserves much more attention than I have space for here. Both were interesting people worthy of deeper exploration. It seems we can find in their lives, both guideposts and warnings. My endnotes might give another writer a starting point to tell their story more thoroughly.

ARGO TUNNEL

The Argo Tunnel is a 4.16 mile (6.7 km) tunnel blasted through the mountains between Idaho Springs and the west end of Central City. It connected to several mines in one of the richest mining districts in Colorado but was *not* considered a mine. Instead, it was designed and driven as a tunnel to transport ore from mines and drain the mines it would serve.

The portal of the tunnel is located at Idaho Springs in the heart of a large, mountainous drainage basin known as Clear Creek. Native Americans had hunted in the area for untold centuries. Unrecorded Spanish explorers had passed through the area quite early, followed by American trappers during the 1700s. Before 1858, however, there were no permanent human settlements in what was considered the western extent of the Kansas Territory.

The Gold Rush to the Plains

William Greeneberry "Greene" Russell, an ex-California "Forty-niner" and a party of 104 prospectors discovered gold along Cherry Creek and the South Platte River in the summer of 1858. The party had ventured about five miles (8 km), into the mountains along Ralston Creek, but had found no deposit of gold worth getting excited about. Nonetheless, reports of their meager finds set off the Pike's Peak gold rush late that year. Auraria became the first settlement, followed soon thereafter by Denver City and Arapahoe City.

Even though winter was approaching, the promise of gold lying on the banks of the South Platte River drew people like a magnet. By Christmas, 1858, there were an estimated 1,000 people raising tents and building cabins near the confluence of Cherry Creek and the South Platte. Except for the winds and whispers from near-frozen creeks, the mountains remained silent.

Who knew there would be pianos and dancing in the mountains before the next winter?

The Gold Rush to the Mountains

Two Forty-niners, one from Missouri and the other from Georgia, heard of Russell's finds on the High Plains and decided to check out the stories for themselves. They were both at Fort Laramie in the Nebraska Territory (now eastern Wyoming) and they both followed similar paths on their journeys south. There is no evidence, however, that their paths had ever crossed before ending up prospecting the very same drainage and finding two separate gold deposits only four miles (6.4 km) apart.[1]

George Jackson of Missouri was the first to set out from Fort Laramie in the fall of 1858. He panned all the creeks flowing out of the mountains as he traveled south and arrived somewhere around Auraria in December. Unlike many of the newcomers, Jackson quickly realized that the gold on the plains must have come from somewhere in the mountains to the west. On January 4, 1859, he set about prospecting Vasquez Fork, later known as Clear Creek, and found that it carried gold. Panning upstream, he encountered a major fork in the ice cold creek about fourteen miles (23 km) from the mountain front. He prospected the north fork about three miles (5 km), but decided to explore the south branch instead. Panning as he went, he kept finding gold. On January 7, Jackson located gold in the frozen gravel of a creek that entered the main branch from the south, about nine and half miles (15 km) above the forks of Vasquez Creek. He marked his spot, retreated to the plains to avoid an impending storm, and waited for the ground to thaw.

Jackson confirmed his discovery in the first week of April, 1859 and after telling people about his discovery down on the plains, set off a new rush to "Jackson's Diggings." The approximate location of his find is marked today by a monument along Chicago Creek, about 200 yards (183 m) south of Clear Creek at Exit 241, off Interstate Highway 70. A small settlement named Sacramento City soon sprung up, later renamed Idahoe and later still, as Idaho Springs.

A week or so after Jackson, John Gregory also prospected Vasquez Fork into the mountains, but at the forks of the creek, decided the north branch was

Monument to George Jackson, a short distance south of Interstate Highway 70 along Chicago Creek and Colorado Highway 103— *Author's photo.*

THE FIRST GOLD DISCOVERIES IN COLORADO

There has long been recognition of earlier gold discoveries in the state, but none attracted much attention. James Pursley found a small gold nugget in 1804 or 1805 and reported his discovery to explorer Zebulon Pike in 1807. There is disagreement in the literature whether the gold came from the South Platte or South Park. Thomas Isern related several stories of gold discoveries in the South Platte Basin during the 1830s and 1840s in his thesis, *The Making of a Gold Rush, 1858-1860*. Louis Ralston and John Beck (later a member of the Russell party) located gold on Cherry Creek and Ralston Creek on their journey to the California gold fields in 1849. Ovando Hollister reported in *The Mines of Colorado* (1867), that a party of Cherokee Indians had also panned a small amount of gold from Ralston Creek on their way to California in 1852. Members of their tribe re-visited the area and recovered gold in annual trips prior to the founding of Denver City.

better than the south. About seven miles (11 km) further up, a small stream entered from the west. Gregory panned north along main creek above that drainage, but noticed that the amount of gold dust in his pan had dropped off. Panning up the small tributary, he passed yet another gulch coming in from the left. He again found a dropoff in gold after he passed it. He backed off and tried panning some dirt from the hillside. A bit further up the hill, he found even more gold and instantly knew he had discovered a gold vein. Like Jackson before him, a heavy April snow also drove Gregory from the mountains. Over the next two or three weeks, he met up with a band of prospectors from Indiana, and together they set out to prove up his discovery. They relocated Gregory's earlier find and on May 6, 1859, staked their first claims.

Up until then, the only discoveries in the area had been placer gold, the gold found in sand and gravel along watercourses. Gregory had discovered the region's first occurrence of *vein* or *lode* gold. Veins were known to be the ultimate sources of gold that ended up as placers. A second gold rush to the mountains ensued, this one bigger than the first. The new gold rush to "Gregory's Diggings" almost emptied the new settlements down on the plains and even attracted some of the latecomers at Jackson's site. By June 1, less than a month after his discovery, there were an estimated 5,000 men in the gulch west of today's Black Hawk. About a half mile (800 m) farther up the gulch was a wide area suitable for settlement which shortly after became Central City.[2] No one in the vicinity was idle.

By July, there were a reported hundred sluices running within a short distance of Gregory's discovery.[3] Brand new towns of Russell Gulch, Nevadaville, and others had sprung up almost overnight. Prospectors spread out like ants. They located hundreds of gold deposits within twenty miles (32 km) of the initial discoveries, but the heaviest concentration of deposits were located within an area only five miles long and three miles wide (8 km x 5 km) By the end of 1859, miners prospected far and wide across the territory, digging mines in areas only native Americans, Spanish explorers, and trappers had ever seen before.

There were no reporting methods or requirements at the time, so it is impossible to know how much gold those early miners pulled out of streams and shallow mines. Best estimates place the number in the range of 640,000 troy ounces (19,900 kg) in just the first ten years.[4] That amount of gold would be worth over 800 million dollars today. That impressive number doubled within only five more years!

Such staggering wealth came at a price. Discovery was utterly random. Development took place without plan. Early extraction focused entirely on mining the best ore first and ignoring almost everything else.

Mining

Gold is never spread throughout the earth uniformly. Most gold deposits in the area around the first two discoveries were concentrated in rich, narrow zones known as veins. Veins can be visualized as underground curtains of mineralized rock. (See the sidebar titled "What are gold veins?", pg. 15.)

In today's world, mining involves exploration, preceded by research into an area's geology and followed by expensive drilling and sampling. Gold prospecting in the 1840s, 50s, and 60s primarily involved a rusty pan, a rifle and a dog, along with a generous helping of luck. The easiest and cheapest part of the mining equation was finding something to mine.

Once promising ore bodies were located, the real work of extraction began. Adits (access tunnels) had to be driven and shafts had to be sunk. Precious metals were locked inside hard rock, so mills had to be built to crush ore to get at the gold.

Price fluctuations cause mining of mineral commodities to be cyclic. That was not the case with gold until 1934, because the U. S. government had tied the dollar to a stable, mandated price of $20.67 per troy ounce (31.1 g) Underground mines in the area extracted around 40,000 troy ounces (1,244 kg) of gold during 1860. Production dropped by about 7,000 troy ounces (218 kg) in 1861, but climbed again for the next four years as more and more mines began operating. Nonetheless, it became more difficult to extract gold each year because the nature of the rock changed with depth. Even though assays (analyses) showed the amount of gold in the rock had not changed much, the ore became more difficult to mill and process.

Mines gradually closed because it cost more to recover gold than it was worth. By 1866, the amount of gold mined was almost exactly the same as it had been in 1863. Salvation for the district appeared in 1868 with the opening of the Boston & Colorado smelting facility in the valley at Black Hawk. With the exception of two years, Gilpin County mines pulled more than 50,000 troy ounces (1,555 kg) of gold out of the ground every year until 1920.

No one has successfully tallied the number of mines that were in the district bounded by the towns of Central City, Black Hawk, Idaho Springs, and Russell Gulch. About fifty would have been classified as major producers with another hundred being "significant" mines. Beyond that, a sheer guess of possibly four

An early horse-powered hoist at an unknown mine, probably in Clear Creek or Gilpin Counties. Hanging from the hoist is a mine bucket. Just beyond the hoist at left appears to be a small oven, possibly for evaporating mercury from *amalgam*. More about amalgam and that dangerous practice later—*Historical Society of Idaho Springs.*

hundred minor mines seems like a fair estimate. The number is hard to determine because mine names changed, mines merged, and not all mines that had been promoted ever saw operation. Moreover, there were 2,000 to 4,000 prospects in the district that never amounted to anything more than a hole in the ground named by their claim holders.

Problems of every imaginable description plague underground mines. Some are little more than nuisances. Some can be catastrophic. Most mines in Gilpin and Clear Creek Counties shared problems with ore, labor, and supplies. And, of course, all mines had incessant money problems. The big three problems, however, were hoisting, excess groundwater, and transportation. They were universal throughout the region and affected almost every mine within a few months of opening for business.

Hoisting

Mining is highly sensitive to economies of scale. It has always been difficult to make money mining on a shoestring budget.

The vast majority of Colorado mines were small, independent operations for the first couple decades. Mines rarely shared hoisting, tunneling, milling, or much of anything. Every mine bought its own equipment and built its own facilities. Independent operation meant few economies of scale, so costs of extracting gold were higher than if multiple mines had cooperated and worked together. Operating costs forced many mines, probably the majority, into abandonment long before they ran out of gold ore.

Lifting ore and waste rock out of mines is one of many unforgiving costs of mining and turns costly in a very short time. Extraction through shafts in the early days of the gold rush was accomplished with ropes, pulleys, buckets, and animal power. Long ropes were available, but ropes did not last long in the wet and abrasive environments of shaft mines.

Once the railroad reached Black Hawk in the 1870s, long and heavy steel cables could be used. Cables had long operating lives and rarely failed. Nonetheless, they were costly and required larger and more expensive hoisting equipment.

Groundwater

One of the least controllable costs in shaft mining is water removal. The longer mines work, the deeper they dig into the earth. If they dig deep enough, all shaft mines reach the water table, the level at which rocks are saturated. The rocks that make up the mountains around Central City and Idaho Springs are minimally absorbent, but the combined volume of water in billions of small cracks and crevices is tremendous.

As shafts sink deeper, the volume and pressure of water increases inexorably. Mines cannot be worked unless water is drained, but drainage is expensive and costs increase with every foot of depth.

The bottoms of shafts in most of the major mines in the region were over five

Three Shay locomotives of the Gilpin Tramway at its yard and repair shop, 0.8 miles north of Black Hawk. General manager Fred Kruse at far left—*Denver Public Library Special Collections, Z-3476.*

WHAT ARE GOLD VEINS?

The Argo Tunnel intersected many *veins* along its length. A few contained gold; most were barren. But what are veins, really?

Gold veins are NOT bands of pure gold. Nor do they course through the earth like veins in the human body. Instead, gold veins are *zones* of mineralized rock that contain minerals, only one of which might be gold. Veins are shaped somewhat like underground curtains of rock.

Most gold veins in Gilpin and Clear Creek counties were formed along fractures in the earth's outer crust during episodes of mountain-building. Those fractures could be short or long. They may have been vertical or tilted. They may have extended downward from the surface a short distance or thousands of feet. The best, real-world examples of how those fractures appear inside the mountains are the fractures seen in concrete sidewalks and driveways, just at a vastly different scale.

Gold mining takes place in cracked and fractured areas of the earth's crust. The crust averages about 25 miles thick and beneath the crust is a hot, semi-solid layer of the earth called the *mantle*. The forces of mountain-building can squeeze hot fluids upward from the mantle into cracks in the crust. Those fluids are much too hot for liquid water, but are made up of silicates and other melted minerals. Sometimes those fluids contain gold, silver, and other valuable minerals.

Those mineralized fluids cool very slowly and form crystalline minerals, usually with appearances different than the fractured rocks through which they pierce. Those mineralized zones are called *veins*.

Fractures in the earth's crust are known in every state in the country, but only a few were mineralized. In fact, mineralized veins are rare and gold-bearing veins are much rarer still.

To the naked eye, even very rich gold veins are normally unimpressive. That is because gold is usually hidden within other minerals and usually discoverable only by analytical tests. When present as discrete particles, gold tends to be microscopic and only rarely visible to the unaided eye.

In the area around Central City and Idaho Springs, mineralized veins range from wafer-thin to twenty feet (6 m) wide and are usually tilted ten to forty-five degrees from vertical. Most mineable ore zones within those veins were only one to four feet (30–120 cm) wide.

Veins may be hard or soft. They may appear banded or unbanded. Veins are often identifiable by differences in texture and color and they frequently display an array of crystalline minerals. Veins often served as avenues for groundwater seepage along the length of the Argo Tunnel. Veins are normally considered worthless unless they contain gold, silver, or some other metal. Even then, they are considered mineable only when mineral concentrations are sufficiently high.

hundred feet (152 m) deep. Some mines were over a thousand feet (305 m) deep and the California Mine near Nevadaville, was the deepest in the region at 2,250 feet (686 meters.) A few mines attempted mechanical pumps, but found that they failed frequently because of acidic mine waters. The majority of mines baled water.

Most mines hoisted water with large buckets, exactly like baling water out of a small boat or canoe. Many mines in the Central City District hoisted water for two working shifts for every one shift spent hoisting ore according to *Mining in Colorado* (U. S. Geological Survey Professional Paper 138).

Under the best of conditions, water control was difficult in the Gilpin and Clear Creek Counties mining districts. Challenges were made worse, often much worse, when neighboring mines shut down. Within a relatively short time, abandoned mines filled with water and became huge underground reservoirs. If abandoned mines were sufficiently large and nearby, active mines were often unable to control water ingress. Removing water from a mine was similar to trying to plug a leaky dam. The deeper the water being held back, the greater the problem. Even mines with large gold reserves succumbed to costly battles against water. As mine after mine surrendered to flooding, water problems caused by abandoned mines closed large areas long before they were worked out.

Transportation

Transportation is yet another huge cost in mining. The greater the distance between a mine and its mill, the more it costs to haul ore. Denver did not get rail service until June, 1870 and the mining area was distant from Denver. The Colorado Central Railroad reached Black Hawk in December, 1872, and supply and travel costs began to drop. The Colorado Central reached Idaho Springs in 1877 and Central City in 1878 and costs dropped further. Even with rail service to the population centers, mines still depended on wagons and animal power to transport ore to mills and then to railheads. Teamsters were happy; miners not so much.

Local entrepreneurs formed the Gilpin Tramway Company in 1866 to lay narrow gauge track (two feet or 61 cm between the rails) from Black Hawk to practically all the major mines in the Central City District. The Tramway reached all the way to the Frontenac and Aduddell Mines in southern Gilpin County within only two years. The Tramway did not reach mines in the eastern part of the district and were consequently hamstrung with expensive wagon haulage. Operating costs were higher in that area, so many of those mines closed before truck haulage appeared after World War I. Some may still hold quantities of higher-quality reserves.

The Tramway served mines with 2-foot gauge track, but the Colorado & Southern Railroad used a 3-foot (91.4 cm) gauge line to connected the gold district to Denver. That meant all inbound supplies and outbound ore needed to be transloaded between cars of different gauges. What if mine cars instead of rail cars could haul ore directly to mills?

How could that be accomplished?

ABBREVIATIONS AND CONVERSIONS

Weight	Distance
g = gram	cm = centimeter = 0.1 m
kg = kilogram (1,000 g) = 2.205 lb	ft = feet = 12 in = 0.3048 m
lb = pound = 456.59 g	in = inch = 2.54 cm
oz t = troy ounce = 31.10 g	km = kilometer (1,000 m) = 0.62 mi
ton = 2,000 lb = 907 kg	m = meter = 39.7 in = 3.28 ft
	mi = mile = 5,280 ft = 1.61 km

Standard American commerce expresses weight in "avoirdupois" pounds and ounces. Rock and ore are measured in tons of 2,000 pounds.

Gold and silver are measured in troy ounces (31.10 g.) This book always spells that measurement to clearly distinguish the difference from ordinary and lighter avoirdupois ounces (28.35 g.)

By digging a tunnel under the mountains. Such a tunnel could access gold veins at great depth. Mine owners could blast shafts *upward* from tunnel level at much less expense than digging shafts downward. Miners could drop ore directly down shafts for free instead of spending money hoisting rock to the surface.

Not only would such a tunnel lower the expense of mining, but it could drain mines at the same time. In fact, a tunnel like that could make it economical to re-open mines that had been flooded for years. Think how much money mines would save! Surely, those mines would be willing to pay a company to drain their mines and haul ore to mills at Idaho Springs. Who knows? Maybe such a tunnel would even discover new gold veins underground that had never reached all the way to the surface.

This was exactly Samuel Newhouse's idea in about 1890.

Turning the idea into reality

Digging a transportation and drainage tunnel through a mining district was not a new idea. There were lots of small tunnels in the area by 1890. Adolph Sutro had pioneered a larger concept in 1878 by driving a 3.9-mile (6.3 km) tunnel into the heart of the famous Comstock Lode of western Nevada.[5] Mimicking the Sutro Tunnel in Colorado seemed simple. All things considered, Samuel Newhouse had only three problems to solve: where to start the tunnel, where to end the tunnel, and where to find the money to pay for it.

The tunnel's destination was somewhat of a foregone conclusion. The northwest edge of the Central City gold district was well established by a cluster of gold veins that started about a mile (1.6 km) due west of Central City. (See the map on page 25.) The cluster of veins trended northeastward

TYPES OF GOLD DEPOSITS

Placer gold is gold dust, gold flakes, and gold nuggets that can be panned or dredged from gravel in creek and river bottoms. (*Placer* is pronounced like "plaster" without the "t.")

Lode gold is found in mineralized veins within otherwise barren rock. Most old engravings depict miners digging with a pick, but mining is really accomplished by drilling holes with drill "steels" and loading those holes with dynamite or explosive gel. (*Lode* is pronounced like "load.")

toward the North Fork of Clear Creek and passed a short distance north of town. The vein system was richest on the west end. The rich Concrete, Grand Army, and Gunnell Mines had been working there since the 1859 gold rush, but had been plagued continually by too much water.[6]

A vein right on the boundary was named the Eureka. The Eureka Mine had acceptably rich ore and promised more ore at depth, It was located 500 feet (150 m) north of the Concrete Mine and Newhouse controlled the Eureka through a lease.[7] What if he dug the Eureka shaft to the level of a proposed tunnel? That would allow him to dig a tunnel from both ends, a luxury that Sutro never had in Nevada. Digging a tunnel from two directions would take less time. The Eureka Mine seemed like the ideal destination for a long tunnel.

Where should Newhouse start a tunnel at the other end? The portal clearly needed to be lower than Central City, and the lower, the better. Ideally, the portal should be close to rail transportation.

Prospectors had examined almost every square inch of Gilpin and Clear Creek counties over the previous three decades. They had staked claims over every crack and lineation in the earth's surface that even hinted of gold or silver. Those old-timers never missed much.

Prospectors had long since discovered that almost every vein in the Central City district trended generally from the southwest to the northeast in a three mile (5 km) wide band. The width of the gold-bearing area varied and veins were never perfectly parallel with each other. Some veins were very long and some were short. Some veins crossed and some veins merged with others. Some were rich in gold, some were rich in silver, and many were barren. And yes, a few veins trended in odd directions. The situation would have appeared chaotic to the lay public, but every local miner, including Samuel Newhouse, already knew where the best gold was located.

Less than two miles (3 km) east of the Eureka Mine was the town of Black Hawk, situated on North Clear Creek. The creek at Black Hawk was about 550 feet (167 m) lower than Prosser Gulch where the Eureka, Concrete, Grand Army, and Gunnell Mines were located.

A horizontal tunnel started from there would head almost due west to reach the Eureka Mine. Along that alignment were only six or eight known gold veins and they had already been heavily mined. To top it off, a tunnel dug west from Black Hawk would be relatively shallow. It was clear that a tunnel driven from North Clear Creek would not be worth the expense.

A better site would be along South Clear Creek near Idaho Springs. A tunnel driven from that vicinity would bore under the entire mining district and would intersect a large number of gold veins at depths approaching 2,000 feet (609 m.) The South Clear Creek drainage was over a thousand feet (300 m) lower than the shafts around Central City.[8] The tunnel needed to slope slightly uphill so it would drain, but would still be over fourteen hundred feet (427 m) below the headframes of the Eureka and Concrete Mines and over eighteen hundred feet (549 m) lower than the California Mine at Nevadaville.

A tunnel started in the vicinity of the Stanley Mine, west of Idaho Springs, would pass directly under the rich gold area of Russell Gulch. If the portal were situated east of Idaho Springs, a tunnel would pass near or under the workings of the Gem, Frontenac, Aduddell, Saratoga, and Sun and Moon Mines. Both portal locations held promise. Idaho Springs would be a perfect starting point.

Funding the idea

Sometime during the 1880s, Samuel Newhouse had cultivated relationships with British investors. Starting in about 1890, Newhouse had interested English investors in placing money into projects around Denver. Although no solid proof has been found, it seems likely he had used similar funds for earlier mining ventures around Ouray and Silverton in Southwestern Colorado. Newhouse had big ideas for his tunnel and those ideas required large investments.

Newhouse had solidified his tunnel plan sufficiently by 1891 to stake out a portal location. Newhouse plainly knew he needed a large space for rock disposal. He found a suitable area along Clear Creek just east of Idaho Springs. The valley at that location was unoccupied and wider than the area west of town. Newhouse subsequently staked two mining claims in that area in February, 1891[9] and began assembling a cadre of British investors, probably around the middle of 1892.

With funding assured, he formed the Argo Mining, Drainage,

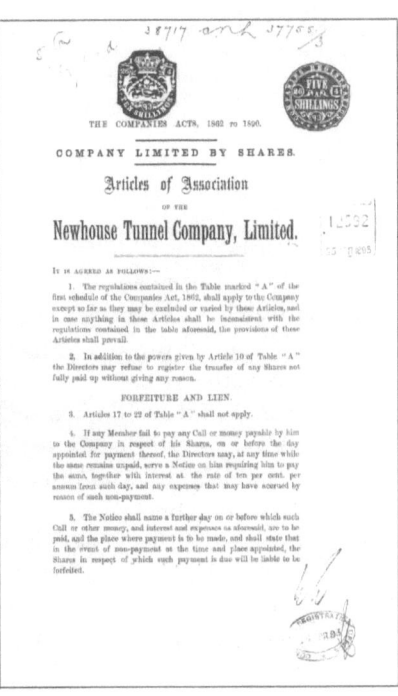

British articles of incorporation of Newhouse Tunnel Company—*The Mighty Argo Gold Mill & Tunnel.*

The Idaho Springs News.
FRIDAY, OCTOBER 20, 1893.

Few of our citizens are aware of the immensity and importance of the enterprise that is being started below here just opposite the old Welch placer—we allude to the new tunnel, called the Argo, that is being started by Mr. Samuel Newhouse of London, England. This tunnel will be run from the starting point on Clear Creek to Nevadaville in Gilpin county, a distance of four miles or over, and will be 7x8 feet in the clear, large enough for the double track that it will be supplied with. A short time since a side track was constructed from the main line of the U. P. to convey the heavy machinery to the mouth of the tunnel. The best and latest improved machinery that can be obtained has been purchased and every preparation is being made to prosecute the work with all the energy and speed possible. A large 100-horse power boiler is already in place and a powerful Norwalk air compressor is expected today. A brick engine house and blacksmith shop is being built 30x35 feet. The plant already purchased and now being erected at the mouth of the tunnel will be duplicated to guard against delays occasioned by the breaking of any portion of that which is in use. Mr. Newhouse says there is money enough now in the "strong box" to to keep the work going for two years. Two air drills will be kept pounding away day and night until the great bore is pushed through to its destination. The line laid out for the tunnel runs through the heart of Seaton mountain and will cut numbers of rich veins, that have been worked at no great depth, at a distance beneath the surface that will prove beyond doubt whether deep mining will be profitable or not. This is not the only object in view for this great undertaking. When completed it will also serve as an outlet for the rich ores of Gilpin county, which will be brought to the banks of Clear Creek where unlimited water power can be had to run mills for its treatment. Mr. Matthew Allan, the gentleman who has immediate control of the work, is an old mining man and is thoroughly competent to carry on the great work to a successful completion.

The Idaho Springs News (Idaho Springs, CO) Oct. 20, 1893—Colorado Historic Newspapers Collection. Colorado State Library.

The first significant mention of the Argo Tunnel project prior to this article had appeared on February 10, 1893 in the same newspaper. That article was short and merely said that Samuel Newhouse, Ancel Newhouse, and Charles Parsons had formed the Argo Mining, Drainage, Transportation and Tunnel Company. No other details were mentioned.

It is uncertain precisely when drilling started in earnest, but an article in Denver's West Side Citizen said the tunnel had progressed one hundred feet by December 15, 1893 and all drilling up to that point had been by hand. It further said that tunneling by air drills would start the following week and would progress at 15 feet (4.6 m) per day. Projections of tunneling progress were overly enthusiastic for a "breaking-in" period. The end of the tunnel was 1,485 feet (453m.) into the mountain by the end of 1894 and progress had actually averaged four feet (1.2 m) per day.

Transportation and Tunnel Company (AMDT&T) January 27, 1893.[10] Three months later, back in London, his investors formed a holding company under British law and named it the Newhouse Tunnel Company, Limited.[11] AMDT&T would be the official owner and operator of the Argo

Blacksmith and machine shops at the portal of the Argo Tunnel in May, 1900—*Historical Society of Idaho Springs.*

Tunnel and the British company would fund the project by purchasing bonds and shares of AMDT&T.

Progress underway

With funding assured, Newhouse began buying equipment in 1893.[12] The exact day tunneling began, is unknown, but the oldest published references[13] suggest site preparation started September 1, 1893. A hand-drawn map from the company at the Denver Public library suggests drilling started in November. Miners managed to construct a portal and blast 80 to 100 feet (24–30 m) of tunnel by the end of 1893.[14] The company switched over to mechanical drills in early January, 1894.

Miners pushed mine cars out the tunnel by hand for the first two months or so.[15] The operation switched over to mule power as soon as the tunnel was solidly under the edge of the mountain and shored up properly with timbers.

From that point until completion, mining industry journals and regular newspapers committed a substantial amount of space to the project. Both Newhouse and his tunnel became celebrities.

21

Argo Tunnel and waste rock dump, probably in early winter, 1898 while progress in the tunnel was purposely halted before reaching the Gem vein—*Denver Public Library Special Collections, CHS-B1512.*

Thirty-four years of earlier mining and claim-staking in the vicinity told Newhouse that it was unlikely that miners would encounter any major gold veins in the first third of the tunnel, but two-thirds of the tunnel would be in an area of previously heavy mining. The great unknown was whether those veins reached all the way down to the tunnel level and whether they would maintain good gold values at depth. Equally unknown was whether Newhouse's tunnel would discover previously unknown veins that never extended to the surface.

The first full year of tunneling was a breaking-in period. Major decisions were made about ventilation, work schedules, blasting techniques, and haulage. Progress averaged about twenty-five feet (7.6 m) per week, so the tunnel was 1,485 feet (453 m) into the mountain by the end of 1894.

"Argo Tunnel" or "Newhouse Tunnel?"

The project was officially named "Argo" from inception, but only a few professional journals used that name in their articles. The vast majority of newspapers and industry magazines preferred the more personal, but unofficial, name of "Newhouse Tunnel." Some persisted in using that name into the 1940s. Perhaps to avoid confusion and for its own promotion, even the Argo company painted buildings with "Newhouse Tunnel." The two names were entirely interchangeable, but 1914 seems to be the approximate dividing line in nomenclature; "Newhouse" prevailed before that time and "Argo" gradually gained popularity after.

Argo Tunnel in February, 1900 showing an expanded waste dump, probably representing 700 to 800 feet of tunnel extension after the previous photo—*Historical Society of Idaho Springs.*

Dig from the Central City end?

With progress underway at Idaho Springs, Newhouse began deepening the shaft at the Eureka Mine.[16] Although he needed to sink the shaft a long way before he reached the level of the proposed tunnel, Newhouse was serious about digging at least part of the tunnel from the northern end.

The Eureka was already an old mine when Newhouse secured his lease on the property. An old miner had owned the property for twenty-five years, but had refused to either work the mine or sell it. Newhouse supposedly spent $50,000 rehabbing the old shaft, deepening it to 600 feet (183 m), and blasting a few horizontal drifts. When the original lease expired, the old man got greedy and demanded substantially larger lease payments plus a large signing bonus.[17]

Conceivably, the mine might have produced enough gold to pay for deepening the shaft an additional 800 feet (244 m). Water removal, however, would have proven an onerous problem until the tunnel was completed. Newhouse ultimately decided the price for the new lease and future costs were too dear.[18] He abandoned his plan of digging the tunnel from both ends and turned his attentions elsewhere.

Stymied progress

Progress in the tunnel increased to thirty-eight (11.6 m) per week during 1895 and forty feet (12.2 m) in 1896. The pace of progress rose to sixty feet

A double-tracked section of the Argo Tunnel at the intersection with the Gem vein. The lateral (or branch tunnel) at right led to workings of the Gem mine. With the air pipe hanging down and the rail switch turned toward the Gem, it is possible this undated photo was taken while the tunnel company paused and waited for the Saratoga mine to help pay for extending the tunnel further—*Historical Society of Idaho Springs.*

(18 m) per week until August, 1897 when the tunnel suddenly shut down a short distance beyond the Tropic vein. Drilling re-started in April, 1898, but shut down again in August. Only ninety-nine feet (30 m) of tunnel had been dug during 1898. What had happened?

Newspapers of the period were entirely silent about the cause of the shutdown. Practically any tunnelling problem could have been cured during that period, so the problem must have been financial rather than technical. Struggling in the absence of corporate confirmation, one writer in later years blamed the shutdown on financial problems suffered by British investors because of some non-existent war between England and Spain.[19]

British shareholders of the Newhouse Tunnel Company voted on February 21, 1899 to reorganize the company as the Argo Tunnel and Mining Company, Limited, also based in London. Exact details are unclear, but with income from transportation still a year away, it is possible that the original company took that opportunity to reorganize its debt.[20]

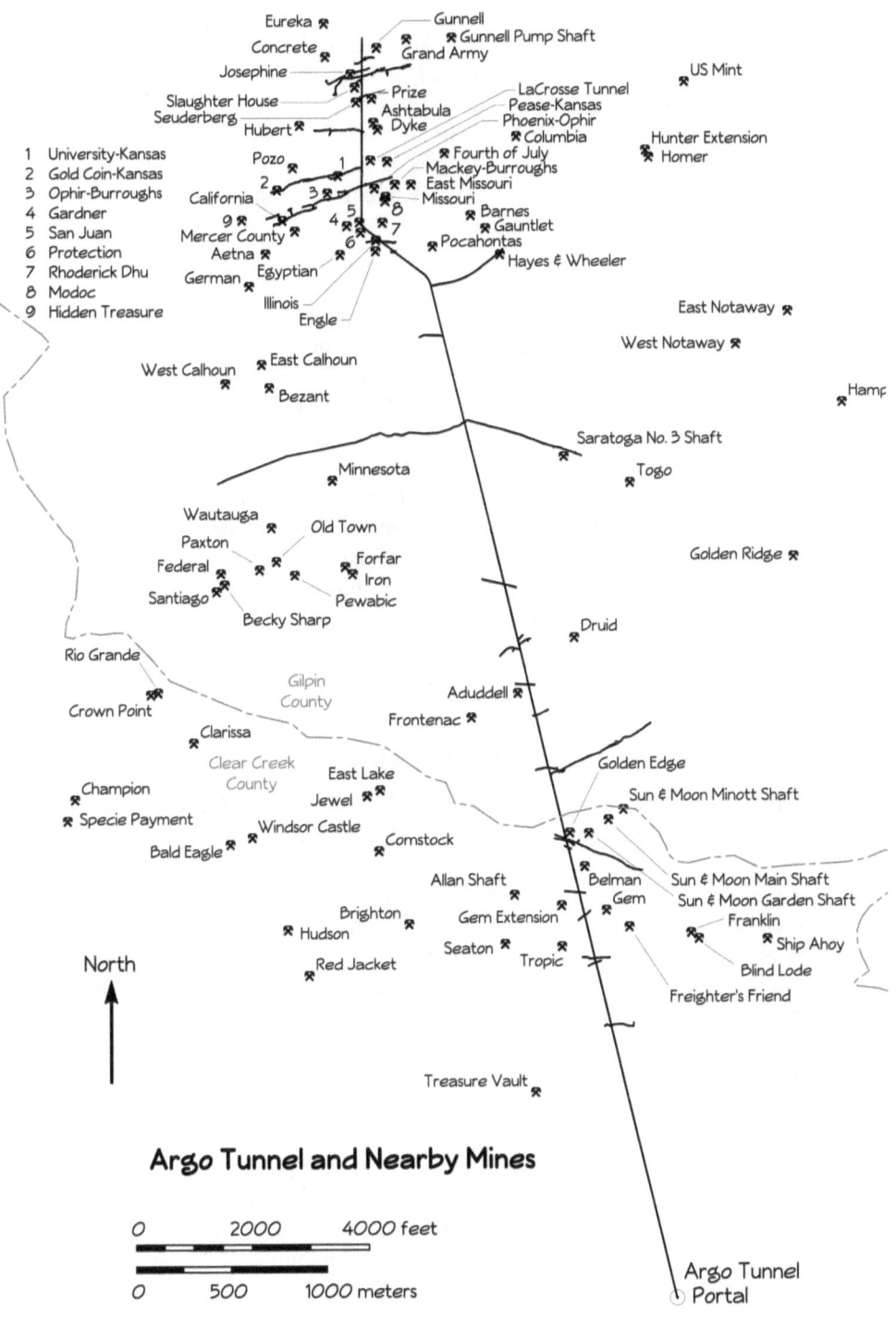

> ## WHAT IS ORE?
> Ore is natural rock that contains at least one useful and valuable element or mineral. Miners consider rock as ore *only* when it can be mined at a profit.
>
> The economic component is important. One mine might be able to make a profit when gold is worth $1,500 per ounce while another might require prices above $1,800. If gold is currently valued at $1,700, one company has ore and the other does not, even though the rock might be identical.

Financial considerations were certainly in play, but one might question why stock and bond holders took over eight months to accomplish the 1899 reorganization. Could forward progress in the tunnel have been halted for a simpler reason? Could tunnel management have been waiting for some sort of financial commitment from a mine beyond the end of the tunnel that was reluctant to pay for drainage?

New funds for tunnelling became available once the new British holding company became operational. At that point, the tunnel had reached 6,718 feet (2,048 m) in length, a distance at which ventilation had become a serious problem. Dynamite explosions gave off noxious smoke and gases, so air in the tunnel needed to be refreshed after each blast. By September, funds allowed installation of a vastly more powerful ventilation fan which allowed miners to blast the tunnel forward another 455 feet (139 m) by the end of 1899.

The first major mines along the way

It took until the third week of April, 1900 to reach the Gem vein at 1.5 miles (2.4 km) in from the portal and 2,200 feet (670 m) below the surface. The Gem vein had proven quite rich near the surface and samples taken at tunnel level confirmed it was equally rich at depth. The Gem shaft was then only 600 feet (183 m) deep when the tunnel intersected the vein. The richness of the vein at tunnel level proved the Gem Mine had over two times more gold reserves at depth than it had mined throughout its entire history closer. That knowledge gave the Gem Mine the ability to raise more money for mining. It also gave hope to the tunnel company that it would acquire a large hauling business.

Management redoubled its efforts at tunneling after passing the Gem vin. Throughout the rest of the year, progress increased to 111 feet (34 m) per week, almost twice as fast as any progress up to that point.

Early in November, 1900, the tunnel had cut through an unimpressive vein later confirmed to be the William Penn vein. That vein turned out to be part of a larger vein system mined by the Sun and Moon Mining Company. It took a few years to drive a *lateral* (an access tunnel off the Argo tunnel) northeast along that vein and then blast a *raise* (a shaft driven up instead of down) to connect to the main shaft. Once connected to the tunnel, the Sun and Moon Mine proved a good source of income for the Argo Tunnel.

Switch to electric locomotives

There were periods of fast progress during 1901, but ever-increasing distance from the portal began to take its toll. Mules were still being used to pull loaded ore cars out of the tunnel, and empties back in. Tunnels like the Argo are driven at slight uphill grades to allow for drainage, but there is only so much a mule can pull even at a low grade before exhaustion. The tunnel was over two and a quarter miles long (3.6 km) in November, 1901 when the company switched over to electric haulage. Powerlines were strung along the roof of the tunnel and sixteen-horsepower locomotives replaced animal power.[21]

The tunnel did not fully abandon mules. Mules were always needed to work in the laterals driven off from the main tunnel. Unless extra rock was removed from the walls, laterals were too narrow and twisty for electric locomotive haulage.

Convincing mines to pay

Almost all costs increased as the tunnel lengthened. The volume of water flowing through the tunnel had increased with every new vein encountered

Postcard by The Albertype Company showing tunnel locomotive and two man-trips. The man-trip on the right has a sign indicating it was owned by the Sun and Moon mine. Date unknown, but probably pre-World War I—*Author's collection.*

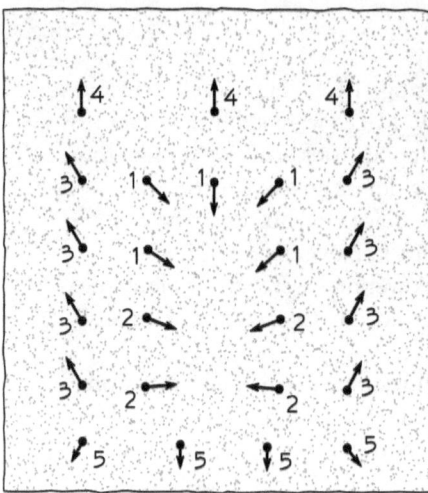

1. Tunnel Blast Hole Pattern
Facing end of tunnel
Numbers indicate blasting order.
Arrows show direction of drill holes.

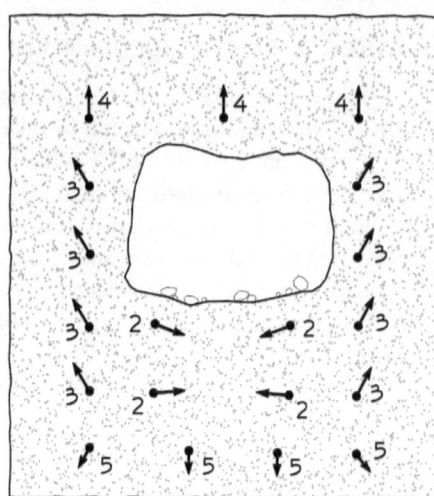

2. Face of tunnel after first blast
"Plunger hole" and "cut holes" exploded and made a cavity in the "face" or "breast" of the tunnel.

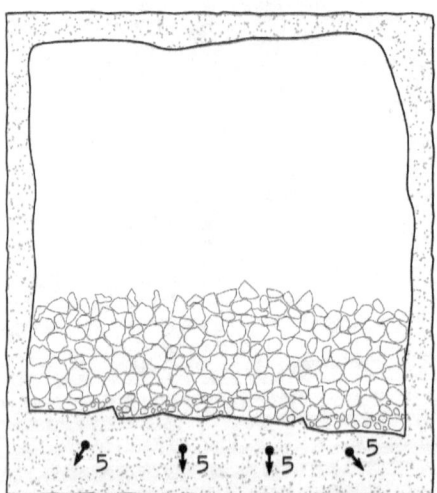

5. Face after fourth blast
"Back holes" brought rock down from the "back" (roof) of the tunnel.

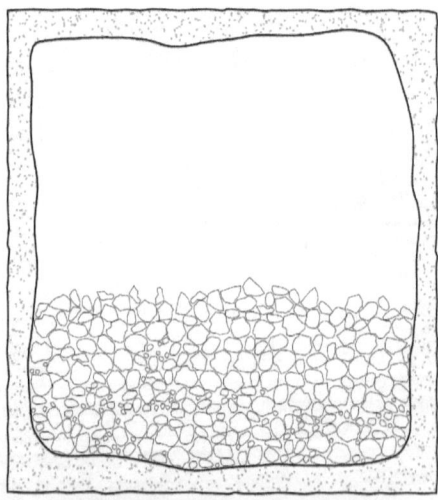

6. Face after final blast
"Lifter holes" removed rock from the "sill" (floor) of the tunnel.

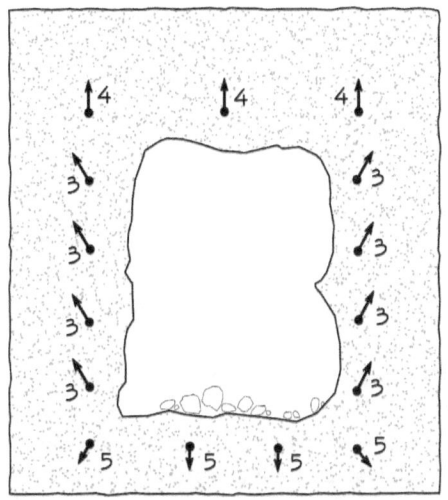

3. Face after second blast
Cut holes enlarged central cavity.
(Cut holes were loaded with more dynamite than other holes and threw most rock outward.)

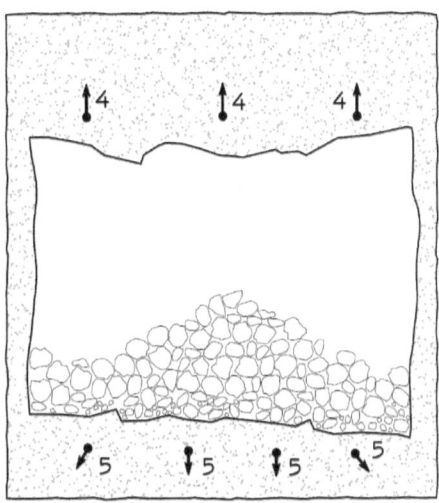

4. Face after third blast
"Side holes" trimmed rock from the "ribs" (walls) of the tunnel.

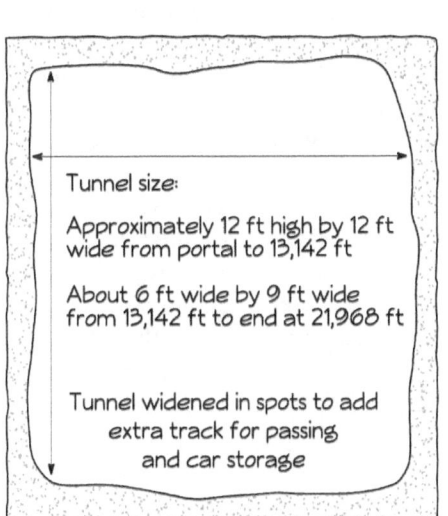

7. Face after "mucking"
Steel plates were laid on the sill to enable faster and easier mucking (removal) of rock.

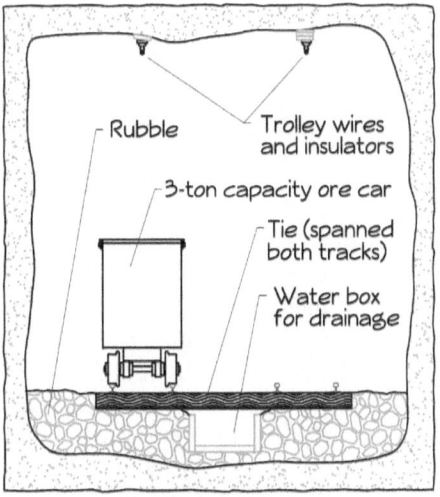

8. Finished tunnel
Leveled and laid with 30 to 35-pound (pounds per yard) rail. Electric locomotives replaced mules in November, 1901.

29

and controlling water meant more labor.

Mines near the tunnel were happy beneficiaries of forward progress in the tunnel. Even though the tunnel was over a thousand feet (305 m) deeper than nearby mines, its presence helped drain their operations. Nonetheless, those mines were reluctant to use the tunnel as Newhouse had intended.

One of the factors that Samuel Newhouse had overlooked was that many mines had already spent money building their own mills, either onsite or near Black Hawk. It made no sense to pay the tunnel company to haul ore out to Idaho Springs and then pay more to load it into railcars and haul it around to Black Hawk for processing. Consequently, fewer mines than expected connected their workings directly to the tunnel. Never mind that many mines were not paying a cent to have the tunnel alleviate their most costly and unforgiving expense–water.

The unwillingness of mines to pay for drainage was becoming a big problem for the tunnel. Possibly a problem that could kill the project!

One can imagine that tunnel management saw bankruptcy on the horizon if it let conditions persist. There had to be a way of getting mines to help pay for tunneling and drainage.

By April, 1902, the tunnel had bored another quarter mile (400 m) under the mountains. The Saratoga Mine was the next major mine on the way toward Central City. Its vein was estimated to be 1,800 feet (550 m) beyond the end of the tunnel. The Saratoga had been one of the richest mines in the district, but also one of the wettest. It had been too expensive to keep the mine entirely dry. Mine engineers calculated that the flooded lower levels held over 300,000,000 gallons (1,135,624 cubic meters) of water.[22] Tunnel management reasoned that it could prevent inadvertently draining the Saratoga Mine by stopping digging in the tunnel. Why spend money driving the tunnel for twelve or eighteen months only to drain a mine that would not pay for drainage or transportation? The Argo Tunnel had leverage and needed to use it. (Explanations had been silent in the mining literature at the time, but it seems nearly certain that the tunnel had previously stopped progress in 1898 and 1899 to force the Gem Mine to pay for drainage.)

Management decided to play the waiting game. From the Argo's perspective, waiting was cheap. It could keep miners busy digging laterals along the Druid, Aduddell, Morning Star, and Wellington veins and those operations could contribute haulage income.

Meanwhile, the Saratoga knew that its vein was aligned to the tunnel at a sharp angle. The Saratoga vein might have been 1,800 feet beyond the tunnel, but parts of the Saratoga Mine were 200 feet (60 m) closer. Maybe the tunnel was already close enough to start draining the mine. The Saratoga Mine also decided to wait.

The Saratoga agrees

It appears both sides negotiated in slow motion. Twenty-five months after suspending work in the tunnel, the Saratoga gave in and agreed to help pay for extending the tunnel to its vein. In turn, the tunnel company agreed to

Two air drills set up to drill the face and extend the tunnel. The tunnel is not as wide as previous photos, so this undated scene is somewhere beyond the tunnel's intersection with the Saratoga vein—*Denver Public Library Special Collections, CHS-B1578.*

narrow the size of the bore in order to save money. Up to that point, the tunnel had been driven ten to twelve feet wide (2.4–3.7 m), twelve feet high (3.7 m) and double-tracked all the way from the portal. Going forward, the tunnel would be narrowed to about six feet wide (1.8 m), nine feet high (2.7 m) and single-tracked. There would still be spots where the tunnel would be widened to accommodate storage of mine cars and passing trains, but tunneling costs would be decreased fifty percent or more.

Tunneling re-started June 20, 1904. With less rock to extract, miners reached the Saratoga vein on February 20, 1905, 14,900 feet (4.5 km) in from the portal. Newspaper articles heralded the success of the tunnel in reaching the vein because it would lower costs at the Saratoga Mine so significantly.

> "Every deep mine in that extremely rich and oldest section of Colorado may be reached either by the main line of the tunnel, or a lateral and forever drained to the level of the bore. When that is done and the expense of pumping is obviated, the ore mined will tax the capacity of every mill in the county to handle it."[23]

That sounded like a great deal for the Saratoga. But what about the tunnel company?

Which mines would step up next?

Management decided to drive the tunnel a short distance beyond the Saratoga vein and the stop progress again on April 15, 1905. Like its previous

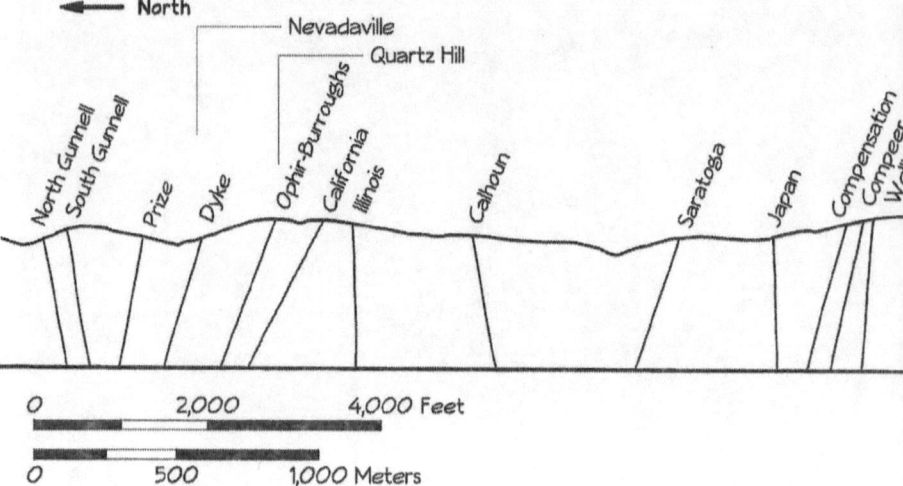

suspension, tunnel management decided to stop digging until similar agreements could be secured from mines further ahead.

Meanwhile, miners began driving a lateral along the Saratoga vein in order to get under the current workings many hundreds of feet above. Forecasts of new transportation business from Saratoga Mine looked great, but they were just predictions. The Saratoga had helped pay for advancing the tunnel, but were other Gilpin County mines further along the tunnel willing to do the same? Did other mine owners think they could outlast the Argo Tunnel? Did they think the Argo Tunnel would drain their operations for free?

Observers in the mining industry were confident that the tunnel would eventually reach its destination, but pundits questioned, "When?" British investors were weary of half-filled promises of profits. In yet another effort to bolster British stock market interest in the project, the Londoners reorganized their holding company for a second time. Whereas, the original company had sold shares for £100 each, and the second company for £1, the new company's shares were to be offered for 10 shillings each or one-half of a British pound.

Investors incorporated a new company in London November 29, 1905 and named it Argo Transportation & Tunnel Company, Limited. Since some tunnel management stayed the same, local newspapers took no notice of changes at the parent company and did not even mention when work resumed in the tunnel early in the spring of 1906.

The Hot Time Lateral

Although seldom immediate, most major mines along its length ultimately connected to the Argo Tunnel through laterals. In concept, laterals operated like the main bore, except that they were never dug as wide or as straight as the main tunnel. The Hot Time Lateral was the most notable of all laterals driven from the Argo Tunnel. Miners drove this lateral west from the same point as the Saratoga lateral. Its objective was the shaft of the large Old Town

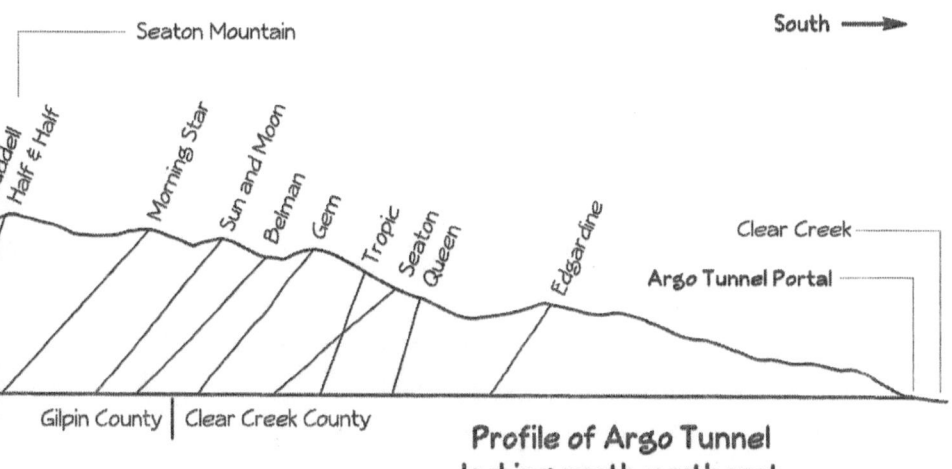

Profile of Argo Tunnel looking north-northeast
showing primary veins encountered

Mine, about 4,000 feet (1,200 m) west of the Argo Tunnel. The Old Town Mine was the heaviest producer near the mining community of Russell Gulch.

Information about Argo's laterals is meager. The Old Town Consolidated Mining Company had incorporated the Hot Time Transportation Drainage &

The caption on the original photograph says this image was taken four miles (6.4 km) into the tunnel. The large air supply pipe and the abandoned tracks leading into a lateral at right suggest this was more likely about 3.2 miles from the portal (5.1 km) at the abandoned Mammoth lateral—*Historical Society of Idaho Springs.*

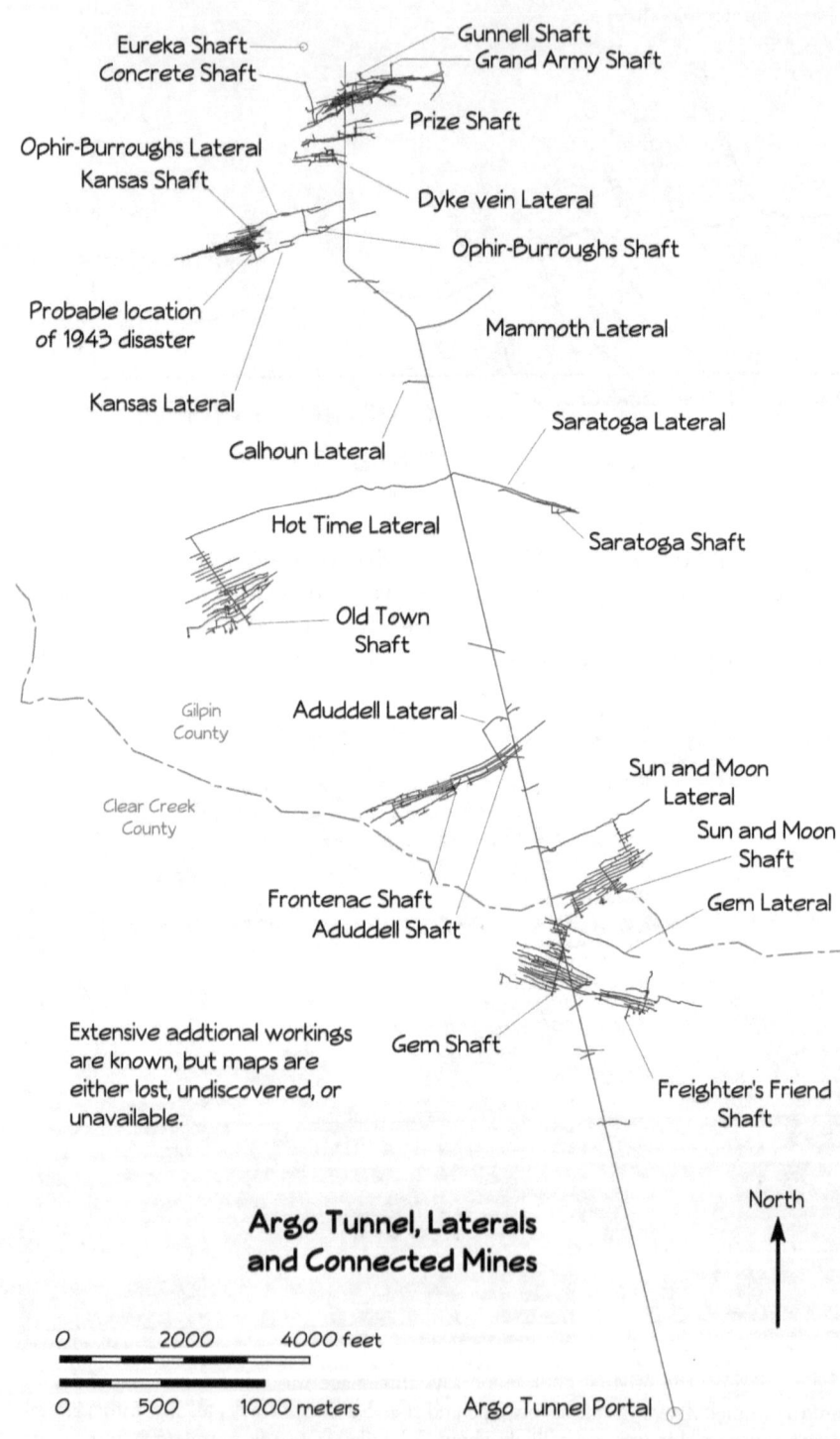

Tunnel Company in 1905.[24] The colorful name originated with the popular 1895 song named, *There'll be a Hot Time in the Old Town Tonight*.[25] Work on the Hot Time Lateral probably started in 1906 and finished in the spring of 1908 at 4,326 feet long (1,318 m), five feet wide and seven feet high (1.5 x 2.1 m). Although never confirmed, it seems likely that the Old Town Mine probably paid a consideration similar to the Saratoga.

The Mammoth Lateral

It took four months to re-start Argo tunneling in April, 1906, but there was no dawdling afterward. Management instituted a bonus system that paid miners extra whenever they extended the tunnel more than two hundred feet (61 m) in a month. Consequently, by May, 1906, miners set a new monthly record and maintained a pace of 275 feet (84 m) per month for the remainder of the year.

Miners were still busy digging the Hot Time Lateral (see map on page 34) when the main tunnel cut a minor vein in mid-January, 1907. Barely mineralized and unimportant by itself, engineers thought that the vein might connect to the Hayes & Wheeler Mine on the east side of the tunnel. As before, management drove the tunnel a short distance past the vein and suspended work a fourth time on February 22, 1907.

A lateral to the Mammoth

The flurry of tunneling during 1906 had been caused by an agreement made with the Gauntlet Gold Mining Company which was particularly interested in driving a lateral from the Argo in order to reach the great Mammoth vein. There was nothing particularly special about the Hayes & Wheeler vein or whether it was the same as the low-grade vein encountered in the tunnel. Gauntlet merely wanted to find some sort of vein in the tunnel, mineralized or not, that could serve as a northeast-trending route along which to drive a lateral toward the Mammoth vein.

The Mammoth vein, also known as the Great Mammoth, had been a very important early discovery in 1859. It was rich and had been worked along the surface for almost 6,000 feet (1,830 m.) Unlike the Gregory and other veins in the vicinity, the Mammoth had proven poor at depth. Gauntlet hoped there might be high-value ore deeper in the vein and could save lots of money by hauling it out the Argo Tunnel.

Miners drove the lateral almost 1,500 feet (450 m) toward the Mammoth vein by the fall of 1908, after which time, reports fell silent in industry publications. A later geologic report said that the lateral had ultimately reached the Mammoth vein, but had encountered disappointingly low gold grades.[26]

A convincing meeting

Only a week or so after suspending work beyond the proposed lateral to the Mammoth, tunnel manager George Collins met with the Gilpin County Chamber of Commerce to explain the future policy of the Argo. Collins' statements at the February 13, 1907 meeting were not publicly reported, but must have been persuasive. In unanimous response, the Chamber issued a resolution:

> "Resolved, that the Gilpin County Chamber of Commerce and citizens of Gilpin County, in mass meeting assembled, do recognize the value of the undertaking as extending the 'life' of the mines of the county, and commend the enterprise of the Newhouse Tunnel Company, and urge upon all property owners along the projected course of the tunnel the advisability of affording it the necessary encouragement by pledging such support as will warrant the completion of the tunnel as a business proposition."[27]

The tunnel was approaching the historically most important veins and mines in the area. The Chamber understood the tunnel's leverage and subsequently talked up the benefits of advancing the tunnel to Nevadaville and beyond. It suggested, in no uncertain terms, that everyone who relied on mining around Central City would benefit if mines signed contracts with the tunnel company.

The 1908 agreement

Drills at the end of the tunnel remained idle for another sixteen months while tunnel management and the Chamber struggled to convince mine owners to help pay for drainage and tunnel development. It did not hurt that the bottoms of several mines were already flooded and mine owners were struggling to keep their mines working at all.

Mine owners close to Central City finally agreed to a deal with the tunnel on May 27, 1908. Most agreed to pay for drainage by a royalty on every ton of gold ore they removed from their mines.[28]

The pertinent details released to the public indicated that mines near the tunnel would pay a fee for every ton of ore extracted ($1 per ton for high-grade ore and 25¢ per ton for lower grade). It did not matter whether ore was hauled through the Argo Tunnel or hoisted to the surface through their own shafts. The agreed-upon fee seems a bit high in retrospect, but was still lower than the cost of dewatering.

Questions remain about that agreement. Did all mine owners agree to pay the fee, or only those in the immediate range of the tunnel's reach during the next year or so? There were hints of fractures in the rosy-sounding agreement,[29] but work resumed in the tunnel soon after signing.

Even with mine owners' agreements in place, British investors decided they were through with the project. The tunnel had become famous worldwide, but investors were tired of repetitive suspensions of tunnel progress and even more fed up with not earning money. In December, 1908, they officially gave up and sold out.

A group of investors from Boston had already owned significant numbers of shares of the British company and were intimately familiar with the Argo Tunnel. They had, in fact, been intimately familiar with Samuel Newhouse

The tunnel company's tall tipple alongside the tracks of the Colorado & Southern Railroad before the mill was built—*Historical Society of Idaho Springs.*

Once the Argo reached its full length and mines along its length began mining in earnest, the waste dump grew substantially. This undated image was probably taken shortly before construction started on the Argo Mill. The dump at this point extended about 1,000 feet (300 m) east of the portal—*Historical Society of Idaho Springs.*

and had invested in his Utah copper projects for years.

Boston investors took over and incorporated a new (and fourth) holding company under the name "Argo Mining and Tunnel Company," but otherwise changed little in tunnel operations.[30]

One of the mines that had touted its early acceptance of the new miners' agreement was the Eureka Mine, Samuel Newhouse's original tunnel destination. A 1906 investment newsletter had commented that,

> "The owners of the Eureka were among the first to contract with the company owning the Newhouse Tunnel. A very reasonable rate was specified for the transportation of ore. Large reduction works will ultimately be built at the south of the Newhouse Tunnel for the treatment of custom ores and this will provide another market for the Eureka output."[31]

The tunnel blasted its way steadily northward throughout 1909. Old mines were drained and re-opened. Several mines quickly started deepening their shafts toward tunnel level. Would mines continue to abide by agreements with the tunnel company?

Waiting for Gunnell

Suddenly, on New Years Day, 1910, work in the tunnel stopped yet again.[32] This time, the tunnel halted a thousand feet (300 m) short of reaching the Gunnell vein. Had the Gunnell Mining & Milling Company refused to sign the agreement? If so, why? The company had significant debts in the form of bonds sold to investors, but it stood to gain more from drainage than practically any mine along the entire length of the tunnel except, perhaps, for the Saratoga. Is it possible that owners of Gunnell did not realize who owned the majority of its bonds?

It was probably not public knowledge, but the Gunnell Mining & Milling Company had not been paying interest on its bonds. And who held those bonds? None other than the same investors who owned the Argo Mining & Tunnel Company. No wonder the tunnel company decided to stop work.

In mid-March, 1910, bondholders foreclosed on the Gunnell company for failing to pay interest as agreed. The bankruptcy court acted promptly, ruled in favor of bondholders, and ordered the sale of Gunnell's mines, claims, and equipment. At foreclosure, bondholders purchased Gunnell's entire mine and assets for $300,000.[33] Since Gunnell's mines (Gunnell, Grand Army, and Concrete) were now owned by the same people who owned the Argo Tunnel, work re-started soon after the foreclosure was finalized.

Completion of the tunnel

Samuel Newhouse, originator of the famous tunnel, had long since moved to Salt Lake City. He had become quite wealthy through the discovery, development, and sale of the Highland Boy Mine. That mine had formed the basis of the Bingham Canyon Mine, the greatest copper deposit known. Nonetheless, he commented on the near-completion of the tunnel project in

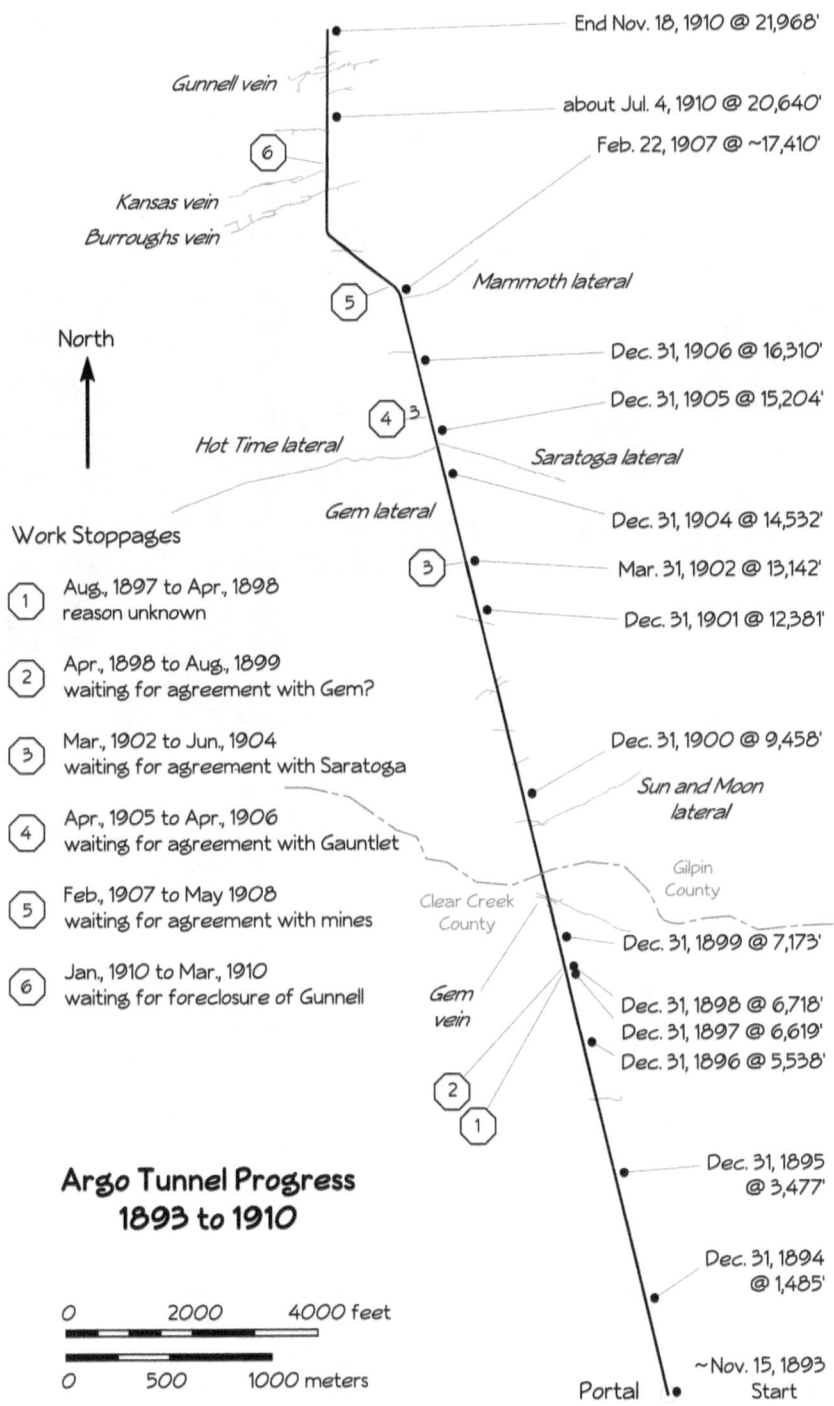

It's rarely sunny when someone wants to show off a big project. Underneath the wooden ramp at the portal was a large air pipe that was later suspended from the roof, suggesting the tunnel was still fairly young. The man seated third from left was Samuel Newhouse, originator and namesake for the tunnel—*Historical Society of Idaho Springs.*

an interview:

> "The tunnel was one of the chimerical ideas of my early days in Colorado. I am still a large holder in that enterprise, although not actively interested, and of course I feel elated to know that the tunnel, which was really a boyish dream, has measured up to most sanguine expectations. Its future will be greater than its past, for we have definitely explored a vast zone of hidden mineral and our work will now be largely devoted to extraction."[34]

No explanation was ever offered in public, but it took twice as long to drive the final 1,000 feet to the Gunnell vein as planned. It appears that ventilation at the extreme length of the tunnel had grown increasingly difficult. Nonetheless, miners shot the last dynamite blast at the end of the Argo Tunnel on Friday, November 18, 1910.[35] Once miners cleared the rock debris and surveyed, the tunnel measured 21,968 feet (4.16 miles or 6.7 kilometers) from portal to end.

By March of 1911, miners had cautiously driven a 200-foot (60 m) raise upwards from tunnel level into the bottom of the Gunnell Mine and drained water away. It was the first time in its 52-year history that the Gunnell was without water problems. Miners cleared away obstructions higher in the mine and enabled natural ventilation through the entire length of the Argo Tunnel.

As the tunnel neared completion, miners in the Eureka Mine could hear blasting in the tunnel several hundred feet below and five hundred feet (150 m) distant. Nonetheless, tunnelling stopped short of the Eureka.[36] By 1910, then-current owners had re-named the operation as the Gilpin-Eureka. The mine was high enough above the nearby drainage of Prosser Gulch that the mine was still dry. Its owners no longer saw reason to fulfill their earlier promises with the tunnel.

> "The present company has not seen the advisability of making a drainage contract with the Newhouse Tunnel in as much as the mine is dry and would in any event be drained by water courses which cross this section. It is quite obvious that it would be more than a mere waste of money, the payment of a useless and unjust tax on the Eureka output to sign a tonnage contract with the Newhouse Tunnel."[37]

It seems obvious that management of the Gilpin-Eureka Mine thought the tunnel was close enough to drain its workings for free. The fact that the Gilpin-Eureka Mining & Milling Co. sold the mine again ten years later suggests they were wrong. When Gilpin-Eureka Mines had Company acquired the mine, its shaft had been dug only minimally deeper than when Newhouse gave up on the project back in the 1890s. Prior to 1920, the newest owners deepened the shaft to 720 feet and planned to deepen it 680 feet further down to tunnel level during 1921.[38] A new financial depression hit the country and probably dried up funds for mining. There is no evidence that the company ever completed its goal and connected to the tunnel. Consequently, like many mines in the district, a significant amount of ore may remain between the bottom of the Gilpin-Eureka shaft and the Argo Tunnel.

Building the mill

Once the Argo Tunnel reached its goal, published reports about the tunnel quickly diminished. The press made only sporadic mentions of the tunnel after 1910. Rock and ore came out of the tunnel in trains as long as 100 cars. Waste rock was diverted onto the huge and growing dump and while ore went to mills around Idaho Springs and smelters at Denver. The tunnel had finally become a business instead of a story.

There were few public comments about the amounts of ore coming out of the tunnel either. By that time, mines all along and adjacent to the tunnel including the Gem, Sun and Moon, Aduddell, Calhoun, Old Town, Prize, Gunnell, Concrete, Grand Army, and several others were shipping ore through the portal at Idaho Springs. For the next eight years, operations at the tunnel became ordinary, barely more interesting than an assembly line of mine cars. Never mind that the Newhouse (Argo) Tunnel had moved more ore through its single bore than any other in Colorado.

There was a ripple of news in mid-1912 with announcements that the "Newhouse Tunnel organization" had formed a company to build a new cyanide mill at the portal of the tunnel.[39] Construction on the mill started in June, 1912 and it opened in April, 1913. but caused little stir. There were already nine mills in the Clear Creek valley near Idaho Springs and some of them had not been paying property taxes. Newsmen were unsure whether the Argo Mill would succeed or not.

Since the new mill was larger than any other mill around in the South Clear Creek Valley, and built on a steel frame instead of wood, the public gradually realized that the Argo Mill was going to be a big deal. The name "Argo Mill" eventually made it into journals and news print in mid-1914. From that point forward, as the Argo Mill became more well known, the "Newhouse Tunnel" moniker gradually gave way to "Argo Tunnel."

The Argo mill had barely been broken in when hostilities of the first World War broke out in late July, 1914. Fighting did not stop until November, 1918. During the intervening period, United States law held gold prices stable, but silver prices rose and helped the profitability of every Gilpin County mine served by the Argo Tunnel. Higher silver prices helped silver mines in Clear Creek County even more.

As the U.S. government sent increasing amounts of armament to Europe, prices for the "base metals" of lead, copper, and zinc grew quickly. The Argo Mill changed its circuitry in 1916 in order to capture more of those metals. By early 1918, copper and lead were accounting for about eight percent of the Argo Mill's payments to mines.[40] That extra eight percent boost proved crucial to many local mines.

The shutdown

That boost in mine profits vaporized almost immediately after European hostilities ceased on Armistice Day, the "eleventh hour of the eleventh day of the eleventh month" of 1918. Once shooting stopped, the United States' vast stockpiles of copper and lead drove prices of those metals into the basement.

While only noticeable in hindsight, the country actually had started sliding into a post-war recession even before hostilities ended. Mines that had been pushed into profitability by strong base metal prices were the first to suffer. By early 1919, it became apparent that mining was doomed for the near term. The Argo Mill held on until April, but too many mines had already turned off their hoists and sent their miners home. There was simply not enough ore to keep mill machinery running on a predictable basis.

One of the largest shippers through the tunnel during the war had been the Tremont Mining Company,[41] a company formed by the Argo Mining & Tunnel Company to work the Gunnell and other mines at the north end of the tunnel. If any company could have survived the recession, it should have been

Electric locomotive pulling a string of empty ore cars into the tunnel past the Gem lateral at left. Intersections with veins like this usually required heavy timbering and cribbing because veins were broken and much weaker than normal wall rocks—*Historical Society of Idaho Springs.*

Tremont. It had good reserves, experienced miners, dry mines, and ready access to the Argo Mill through the tunnel. Even Tremont could not maintain profitability and sputtered along.

The recession eased a bit during the summer and fall, but 1919 turned out to be a terrible year for mining in Colorado. Late in the year, the national economy reversed again and a full-blown depression developed that lasted through July, 1921. Colorado mining companies, including the Argo Tunnel and Mill, were suddenly on sale at steep discounts. The Argo's Boston owners decided to give up like British investors before them.

Revival?

The Gem Mining Company, a consolidation of the Gem, and several adjacent mines, had been formed by Canadian and American investors in July, 1920.[42] Even in the face of the national depression, that company intended to become a major player in the mining business around Idaho Springs. The Gem was the first company with the financial wherewithal to make an offer for the Argo properties in November, 1920. Industry journals reported a purchase price of $250,000,[43] but private papers of George Collins at the Denver Public

43

Library suggest the actual price was closer to $150,000.

It seems likely that the Gem company spent at least part of the remaining $100,000 refurbishing the Argo Mill and increasing its capacity. Investors had formed yet another new company, the Gem Tunnel Company,[44] to operate the tunnel separately. Was there going to be a new boom period of production from Clear Creek and Gilpin Counties? Articles in industry journals certainly made it sound like that.

Many hundreds of employee time slips from the Argo Tunnel and Mill survive. Their sheer numbers suggest substantial work at the tunnel, mill, Gem and Gunnell mines throughout the 1920s. Unfortunately, no production records from that period are known that to confirm actual output.

Time slips and ore receipts suggest renewed activity at the mill and tunnel in 1921, but other sources tell an oddly different story. The Colorado Bureau of Mines said in its *Annual Report for the Year 1921* that, "There were a great many small scale operations in Boulder, Gilpin and Clear Creek counties, but the production as a whole was very small." The Bureau did not even mention Gilpin and Clear Creek Counties in 1922. By 1923, increased industrial production during the "Roaring Twenties" was solidly under way, but the only mention of mining in cunties was that mines needed to ship their products to Leadville because the last remaining smelter in Denver had closed.

For all its development work during 1921 and 1922, the Gem Mining Company succumbed to the undertow of market conditions and expenses. Perhaps the company had increased the capacity of the mill to the point where it could not operate profitably without a large and consistent supply of ore. Shipping heavy concentrate to Leadville, either by truck or rail would have been onerous at best.

Life support

Information about mill and tunnel operations after that period are nebulous. It is known that twenty-two men were employed in the tunnel during 1926, all dedicated to re-timbering and cleanup. By October, that work had ceased.[45] The apparent owner at that time was The Burroughs Pool Mining Company and its miners were employed by Thorn & Sparks, a contract mining company.[46] When an inspector for the state's Bureau of Mines visited the tunnel in mid-1927, he found four men working for a company called the Colorado Gold Corporation. The mill was closed and the only work was re-timbering and cleanup in the tunnel. By Fall, even that work had also ceased.[46]

A different company, Quartz Hill Mining Company, is known to have conducted some work in 1929, presumably in the Gunnell mines. Two years later, the state inspector recorded the tunnel's operator as Chain O' Mines, Inc.,[47] a company with large holdings around Central City. That company officially acquired the tunnel, mill, and mines on January 5, 1932.[48] Mining inspector records list later operators (probably lessees) as Galli Mining Company (1933), King Kong Mines (1935), and Union Carbonate Mines, Inc. (1936).

Collins to the rescue?

California-Hidden Treasure Mines Co. acquired the Argo Mill in 1937 and seems to have been more seriously interested in rehabilitating the tunnel and mill than most of its predecessors. In April, 1938, it acquired 19,997 shares of the 20,000 shares issued by the original Argo Mining, Drainage, Transportation and Tunnel Company through some sort of court judgment.[49] Although confirmation has not been found, it seems probable that the three missing shares were "founder shares" held in the estates of Samuel Newhouse, Ancel Newhouse, and Charles Parsons. That is assuming the shares had not already been lost or destroyed.

George Collins had been a manager and mining engineer for the tunnel company back when it was under the control of Boston interests. During the intervening years, Collins had acquired a large holding of mining properties in Gilpin and Clear Creek counties including control of mines on the rich California-Hidden Treasure vein. Among his portfolio of properties were claims on the Kansas vein at Nevadaville.

The Kansas vein had been discovered during the 1859 Gold Rush. It was a particularly rich vein and was ultimately developed by several competing

View of Nevadaville with the hoist house of the Kansas mine in the foreground. Mines visible on Nevada Hill beyond include (left to right) Golden Treasure, Hubert, North Hubert, Slaughterhouse, and Prize. These mines shipped ore through the Argo Tunnel and processed through the mill. Undated but probably mid-1880s—*Denver Public Library Special Collections, L-36.*

45

companies along its length. At a point 18,360 feet (5,596 m) in from the portal, a lateral had been driven west from the Argo Tunnel along the Kansas vein.[50] Collins knew there were vast amounts of gold remaining deep within that vein.

The Kansas vein and disaster

Sometime between 1937 and 1943, Collins' miners had cleaned out the tunnel sufficiently to get drills, air, and equipment into the lateral somewhere beneath the Kansas Mine. The area was dripping wet. That warned Collins and his miners of a huge reservoir of water above their heads. The million dollar question was the size and depth of that reservoir. A pool twenty feet (6 m) deep would not have been a big problem. A reservoir two hundred feet would have been much worse. A thousand-foot (300 m) deep lake would have been a monumental threat.

Every miner who ever worked in an old mine knew the threat of accidentally drilling into a flooded mine. Pent-up water could be drained, but needed to be released slowly and cautiously. There had already been one local disaster back in August, 1895 at Black Hawk. At that time, fourteen miners had perished when a blast in the Americus Mine breached a rock wall into a flooded section of the Fisk Mine.[51]

Elsewhere in the Argo Tunnel, miners had encountered perched reservoirs of water several times as they drove raises upward from tunnel level into the bottoms of old mines. Miners usually probed ahead carefully with long drill steels when working in wet conditions under old mines. Blasting was always highly cautious. Breaking loose another killer flood was always on their minds.

Unfortunately, experience, foreknowledge, and fear were insufficient for miners on Monday, January 18, 1943.

World War II was raging in Europe, but the fear deep within the Argo Tunnel that day could not have been higher than if miners had been facing enemy machine guns. Several miners had already quit over threatening conditions below the Kansas Mine. It is a wonder anyone volunteered to run a drill or load a stick of dynamite while working in such a veritable waterfall.[52]

At its heart, the plan was obvious. Drain water from the Kansas Mine in a slow, measured manner. Remove only enough rock from overhead to increase water flow. Then, wait for weeks or months for the mine to dry out. There was no need to be in a hurry with such a monstrous threat overhead.

Sadly, no one survived to tell what really happened that day. Retired miner Merle Sowell, in his book, *Historical Highlights of Idaho Springs: Mining Camp Days*, says the disaster was the result of a short-timed dynamite blast. That speculation was supported by the Colorado Bureau of Mines in its 1943 Annual Report.

Other experienced mining people have suggested it would have been madness to have been anywhere near an armed dynamite charge beneath a flooded mine. They have suggested that drilling might have penetrated just far enough to trigger a sudden rockburst. Regardless of causation, the release of hundreds of feet of water from above was catastrophic.

The explosive release of water was stupefying. The torrent that swept downward from the Kansas Mine, through the lateral and out the portal carried mine cars and tons of rock along with it.

The force of the flood was so great that it ripped up heavy rail in the main tunnel. In places, the rail was bent into rusty pretzels weighing hundreds of pounds. A few lengths of twisted rail still lay between the portal of the Argo tunnel and the top of the Argo mill as testimony to the force of the flood.

It took four days before rescuers recovered the bodies of Lewis Hamilton (age 22), Claude Albert (age 30), Charles Bennett (age 56), and Samuel Mettras (age 58).[53]

Damage to the tunnel was devastating. Kelsey Enterprises employed twenty-eight men to clean out the tunnel in 1954, but efforts were quickly abandoned.[54] George Groves, another contractor, tried later that same year, but again abandoned the job.[55]

WAS THE ARGO TUNNEL SUCCESSFUL?

The Argo Tunnel successfully extended the life of the Central City mining district for forty years or more. Together, the Argo Tunnel and Argo Mill directly and indirectly created and saved thousands of mining and support jobs.

Tunnel ownership changed four times in less than sixteen years, so one could reason that the tunnel was not particularly successful at making money for its owners. It took seventeen years to complete the tunnel with six and a half years of idle time waiting for mines to agree to pay for drainage.

Samuel Newhouse and his initial investors had founded their project on the premise that mines would gladly pay to ship ore through the tunnel to mills around Idaho Springs. More importantly, Newhouse predicted mines would trip over themselves to pay the tunnel to de-water their mines.

Make no mistake; many hundreds of thousand of tons of ore and rock moved through the tunnel. Nonetheless, drainage was tremendously more important than haulage to most mine owners. One can only imagine how profitable the tunnel might have been had Newhouse, and his successors, devised an effective method of charging for water removal before blasting forward.

Ironically, the least appreciated long-term benefit of the tunnel was one no one could have imagined in the 1890s.

Ores throughout the district were rich in sulfides. As those sulfides oxidized and the sulfur combined with water, they formed weak sulfuric acid which leached heavy metals and contaminants from ore zones and surrounding wall rocks. Much of that acidic, mineralized water now flows out the Argo Tunnel and into its treatment plant. Without the tunnel and treatment plant, those mine waters would have leaked from seeps and springs spread across mountainous terrain. Mitigating such widespread pollution today would have been a logistical and financial nightmare.

Some of the heavy rail and tunnel cars twisted and bent by the force of flood waters that tore through the Argo Tunnel in 1943 after blasting into the bottom of the deep Kansas mine. Wreckage was hauled out during one of the abandoned cleanout attempts— *Author's photo.*

Contractor Thomas Oetter seems to have attempted the final cleanout in March, 1955. A state mining inspector halted work when he found Oetter and a helper working 4,000 feet (1,200 m) into the tunnel without any ventilation. The inspector commented that a candle *failed to burn beyond 2,500 feet!* (760 m) Oetter and his helper had been able to work only by breathing from medical oxygen bottles.[56] No record of subsequent cleanout work is known.

Superfund cleanup

There has been no natural ventilation through the tunnel since the 1943 disaster, but the tunnel still serves as a drainageway for groundwater. Blockages exist within the tunnel and its many connected mines, but groundwater is in constant motion through unknown miles of old workings. That water dissolves iron, lead, and other contaminants on its way to and through the Argo Tunnel. During that journey, water becomes acidic, stained, and harmful to aquatic life downstream.

Environmental pollution was once considered the price of progress. By 1970, environmental awareness had grown to the point where the federal government created the Environmental Protection Agency (EPA) in an effort to keep the country's pollution from getting worse. The government enacted the *Superfund* law in December, 1980 under the Comprehensive Environmental Response, Compensation and Liability Act (CERCLA). It mandated the EPA clean up polluted sites, starting with the most toxic.

Earlier that same year, the Argo Tunnel had belched a huge discharge of polluted water and mud from its mouth, although the exact cause was never learned. The "blow-out" released so much acidic water into Clear Creek that the City of Golden had to close its water supply intakes for several days. Water users further downstream were affected for several days thereafter.

The EPA created its first four Colorado Superfund sites in September, 1983, among them the "Central City–Clear Creek Superfund Site." The site encompasses 400 square miles (1,035 km^2) around Central City, Black Hawk and Idaho Springs. Several pollution sources were identified within that area, with the Argo Tunnel labeled as the largest single source.

Water flowing from the Argo Tunnel contained elevated levels of cadmium, copper, iron, lead, manganese, and zinc, so water treatment became a top priority. The EPA subsequently built a $5,000,000 water treatment plant a short distance from the portal. The plant became operational in 1998 and was further upgraded in 2012.

The treatment plant was designed to clean water at the rate of 700 gallons (2.6 m^3) per minute. Most of the water comes from the Argo Tunnel with the remainder collected from Virginia Canyon, west of the Argo and the Big Five Tunnel located at the west end of Idaho Springs.

With knowledge of the 1980 discharge still fresh in the Agency's memory, the EPA studied ways of protecting against another unpredictable blow out. It wanted to prevent fish kills and protect downstream water providers, but it

2022 photograph of the massive bulkhead installed by the EPA in 2015 for prevention of damage from a large, unforeseen discharge of acidic and mineralized mine waters— *Author's photo.*

GILPIN AND CLEAR CREEK COUNTIES

Gilpin County was organized around John Gregory's discovery when Colorado became a territory in 1861. Until Broomfield County was formed in 2001, Gilpin was the smallest county in the state. Nonetheless, it led all other counties in gold production until 1893, when overtaken by Teller County and its huge gold telluride deposits at Cripple Creek and Victor. Gilpin County still holds the #2 position.

Clear Creek County was formed at the same time, encompassing most of the South Clear Creek basin, including Jackson's discovery on Chicago Creek. While gold production was significant during the first ten years, Clear Creek was much more famous for silver. For nineteen years, tiny Clear Creek County led the state in silver production until surpassed by mines around Leadville (Lake County) in 1878 and then Aspen (Pitkin County) in 1889. Leadville ultimately produced almost half of all silver mined in the state, but Clear Creek County still holds the #3 rank in silver production.

---

also needed to protect its treatment plant from physical damage. The EPA ultimately decided to install a thick reinforced concrete bulkhead inside the tunnel that now serves as a flood control dam. The Agency could not block the tunnel completely because acidic waters would merely back up until they started leaking out elsewhere.

Contractors completed designs in 2014. A mining contractor installed the bulkhead the next year at a total cost of $1,373,500. Visitors to the site may see the bulkhead 109 feet (33 m) inside the portal. In the middle of the concrete face is a 36-inch (0.9 m) manway through which professionals may inspect the upstream side of the bulkhead when necessary. The bulkhead is about 10 feet tall, 10 feet wide and 5 feet thick (3x3x1.5 m.) The current walkway conceals a few feet of the bottom part of the bulkhead.

A 12-inch (30 cm) corrosion-resistant pipe carries water from behind the bulkhead to the water treatment plant. Workers in the plant monitor and control water flow and water storage behind the bulkhead.[57]

Tunnel statistics

Researchers will find substantial and pervasive disagreement among historic references concerning every statistic and so-called "fact" about the tunnel. The tunnel has been blocked since 1943, so there is no way to confirm or dispute any single measurement or observation. Details in the following table represent the predominance of evidence found in mining literature about the project. Details in newspapers should always be considered approximate and possibly suspect.

In the mining business, experience, technology, mining methods, regulations, rock conditions, and finances are always changing, so almost every

Width, 0–13,142 ft (4,006 m)	8–12 ft	2.4–3.7 m
Width, 13,142 ft to end	6 ft	1.8 m
Width of laterals	3–4 ft	0.9–1.2 m
Height, 0–13,142 ft (4,006 m)	9–12 ft	2.7–3.7 m
Height, 13,142 ft to end	9 ft	2.7 m
Height of laterals	6 ft	1.8 m
Length of main tunnel	4.16 miles	6.7 kilometers
Tunnel and all laterals (estimated)	15–16 miles	24–26 kilometers
Maximum depth from surface (est.)	2,500 ft	762 m
Elevation at portal (est.)	7,543 ft	2,299 m
Depth at end of tunnel (est.)	1,300 ft	396 m
Grade (0.42%–0.5%)	5–6 in/100 ft	0.42–0.5 m/100 m
Construction period	approx. Nov. 1, 1893 to Nov. 18, 1910	
Elapsed construction time	6,277 calendar days	
Construction days (estimated)	3,796 work days	
Construction cost (estimated)	$1,000,000 (per industry literature)	
Active period, continuous	Nov 1, 1893 to Mar 31, 1919	
Active periods, sporadic	Apr,, 1919 to Jan. 10, 1943	
Cleanout attempts, sporadic	Jan., 1943 to Mar., 1955	
Rail gauge	18 in	45.7 cm
Track configuration, double track	13,142 ft	4,006 m
Track configuration, single track	8,826 ft	2,690 m
Track weight, main tunnel	30–35 lb/yard	14.9–17.4 kg/m
laterals, unknown but lighter	variable	variable
Distance between tracks	24 inches	60.96 cm
Drainage ditch	24 in wide between tracks in double-tracked sections and against east wall beyond	
Motive power:		
hand, Nov., 1893–Jan.,1894	0–100 ft	0–30 m
mule, Jan., 1894–Nov., 1901	0–12,100 ft	0–3,688 m
locos, Nov, 1901–Jan., 1943	0–21,968 ft	0–6695 m
Locomotives		
two 16 hp Baldwin-Westinghouse	7 tons	6,350 kg
others, types unknown	unknown	unknown
Tunnel cars, volume	52 ft³	1.5 m³
Tunnel cars, capacity	3 tons	2,721 kg
Mine power	500 volts DC	
Drilling method	by hand Nov, 1893–Jan., 1894 Leyner air and water drills thereafter	
Blasting, dynamite per round	100–175 lb	45–79 kg
Advance per round, approx.)	9–10 ft	2.7–3.0 m
Fusing	electric	

statistic about a mine or tunnel is subject to change over time. It is important to understand that historic reports were often infused with bias to make mines, mills, tunnels, ores, projects, and management seem better or worse than they really were. Consequently, most historic reports about the Argo Tunnel should be considered well-intentioned, but *not necessarily 100% true* at the time they were written.

Fatalities

Mining and tunneling remain dangerous professions. The Argo Tunnel was not immune to injuries and deaths.

January 7, 1902—Two men died instantly while a five-man powder gang was tamping dynamite in a blast hole. A third died later as a result of injuries.[58]

November 1, 1905—One miner suffered a compound leg fracture when his trolley car jumped the track in the tunnel. He died two weeks later from complications.[59]

August 24, 1910—Two miners were electrocuted and two others were slightly injured when their mule-drawn mine car hit two live wires hanging down from the roof of the tunnel.[60] A different report of the accident says the men were electrocuted while trying to rescue a mule that had become entangled in live wires.[61]

January 18, 1943—Four miners drowned as a result of a catastrophic rock failure while working in a raise between the Kansas lateral and the water-filled Kansas Mine above. (See page 46.)

ARGO MILL

The Argo Mill and local mining

The Argo Tunnel reached its maximum length in 1910, by which time it had drained most mines along its length. Mines were deepening their shafts to recover more gold, whether they planned to ship through the tunnel or not.

Water problems were under control and mines were free to extract ore from previously inaccessible reserves. Mining costs had not necessarily risen drastically over the previous two decades, but every penny of increased cost had cut into thin profit margins while the U. S. government had maintained its fixed price of gold at $20.67 per troy ounce (31.1 grams.)

All mines faced the burden of maintenance and refurbishment, of course, but many also needed to replace their old mills. It had been customary throughout the history of the district for mines to build their own mills to process their own ore. Moreover, there were hundreds of mines.

> "...Mills are strewn along the river banks and up the mountain sides in such profusion as to suggest the visitation of epidemics of mill construction."[62]

Every mine owner faced the uncertainty of how long their gold deposits would hold out. There was a possibility that gold veins would pinch and disappear after the next dynamite blast. It was equally possible that the nature of a mine's ore could change with depth and distance from the top of its shaft. Consequently, mine owners seldom built mills for longevity.

To accommodate that universal uncertainty, several "custom mills" had been built in Gilpin County and at least seventeen more had been built in and near Idaho Springs. The term *custom mill* is somewhat confusing. In the mining business, a custom mill is one designed with machinery and processes to enable it to treat ore from several mines. Although not necessarily part of the definition, most custom mills purchased ore from mines versus milling ore and returning concentrates to mines. Custom mills based their offers on how much gold and silver they calculated to be in the ore they bought. The always factored in anticipated losses and processing difficulties.

Mills dedicated to processing ore from single mines could, theoretically, recover more gold and silver than custom mills. That did not mean dedicated mills could respond when the nature of ores changed with depth or distance from shafts or portals. Nor does it mean small mines could afford to build, maintain, and staff their own facilities.

Once the Argo Tunnel was complete and fully operational, management decided it was time to build a large, permanent custom mill at the portal. Such a location featured an inexhaustible supply of water from South Clear

Local newspapers commented that construction on the Argo Mill started in June, 1912. Although undated, this photo was probably taken around October and shows the steel frame had already been erected. The mill started receiving ore and sampling in February, 1913. It had 125 tons (113 tonnes) of ore on hand by the first week of April and gradually started processes in stages. News media declared it operational by the 19th—
Historical Society of Idaho Springs.

Creek, a reliable supply of labor from Idaho Springs, and rail access to smelters at Denver.

The purpose of the Argo Mill

Custom mills like the Argo were highly crucial to success in the gold and silver mining business. At first blush, it appears that the gold mining business combines several separate endeavors: prospecting, mining, milling, and smelting. Most businesses also face challenges of marketing, but there has never been a need for marketing when selling gold.

Of course, few businesses are as simple as they first appear. Every step in producing gold has its share of problems. Take smelting, for instance. A mine could have ore with the richest gold content in the world, but without a method of separating gold from rock, its ore would be worthless.

Smelting relies heavily on science, chemicals, and lots of heat, but is almost as much art as science.

Low-grade ore has always posed a persistent problem for smelters. The lower the amount of gold in ore fed into smelters, the greater the percentage that is lost.

By 1910, the gold and silver districts of Gilpin and Clear Creek counties were over a half century old. New discoveries of high-grade smelting ore were going to be rare. There were certainly pockets of high-grade ore left, but the majority of future ore sent to smelters would probably be lower in grade than what had been mined before.

Consequently, mines always faced the question of whether they could make profits mining low-grade ore.

The answer was normally to send high-grade ore directly to smelters and send the rest to mills. The goal of mills was to remove as much worthless rock as possible, before forwarding *concentrates* to smelters.

With the exception of gold recovered from placer deposits, the very best ore that had ever been mined in the region was more than 99.9% worthless rock! Consequently, if a mill could remove most of that worthless rock, the material that remained would have a much higher gold content.

Milling fits into the gold business between mining and smelting. The only question is whether mines needed to mill ore themselves or pay other companies to do it for them.

Removing worthless rock from ore is not simple, nor are mills.

A mill is a puzzling part of the mining business. Borrowing a saying attributed to Winston Churchill, a mill is "a riddle, wrapped in a mystery, inside an enigma."

The Argo Mill is definitely an enigma to first-time visitors. It is a big box that holds a collection of crazy-looking contraptions that seem to make no sense. They are contrivances that most people have never seen before and will likely never encounter anywhere else.

The simplest way to understand the Argo Mill and its machinery is to realize that everything in the building contributed to one central purpose: **remove stuff that was not gold.**

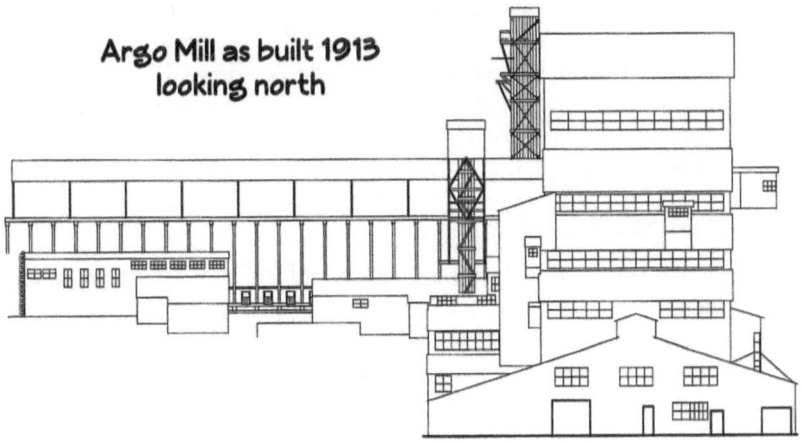

Argo Mill as built 1913 looking north

Undated photograph show gondola cars parked on the siding at the Argo Mill. The cars appear to be loaded with light-colored ore. The image possibly dates from 1917 or 1918 when light-colored silver ore was being shipped from Empire, Georgetown, and Silver Plume. There are no signs of dilapidation commonly seen in later photographs—*Historical Society of Idaho Springs*

Most machines in the building had separate purposes, but none worked alone. Every machine depended on others in some manner and all worked together to form one large, "big box" machine called the Argo Mill. Its purpose was to remove worthless material from raw or "mine run" ore. Low- and medium grade ore entered at the top and high-value concentrate exited at the bottom ready for shipment to a smelter for refinement. Its purpose was to reduce large volumes of ore into smaller, richer quantities.

The Argo Mill was a custom mill so it could not depend on a single mine for its livelihood. It could survive only by buying ores from several mines. Hence, the official name of the company that built the mill: The Argo Reduction and Ore Purchasing Company.

The Argo Mill business

It is easier to understand how the mill worked by first grasping the intent of the business.

Take a few minutes to step back to 1912, into the role of the owners of the Argo Tunnel. At that time, the tunnel company was charging to haul gold ore out of the tunnel and to haul mining supplies back in. It was charging for draining water away from mines. The business was profitable enough to pay its bills, and employees and it was paying some dividends to investors. Truthfully, no one was going to get rich. It might have been a different story if all the mines that benefitted from the tunnel had been willing to ship ore through the tunnel as Samuel Newhouse had planned, but there was no way to turn back the clock.

Yes, the company charged to haul ore. But so did the teamsters and the railroad that transported ore to mills elsewhere. It was disappointing for tunnel owners to watch all that ore put money into the pockets of other businesses. Why not build a mill just outside the portal and process the ore right there? How would one go about designing a mill?

The first step is to start asking questions, as many questions as possible. Then answer those questions and organize them in sensible order.

An excellent question to ask is, "Where could a mill sell gold?"

The best place to sell gold would have been the United States Mint in Denver. By law, the mint paid full value for whatever gold it purchased. However, it bought only very high-grade material like nuggets, placer gold, gold bars, impure bullion and high-grade ore.

It was already a foregone conclusion that such a mill at the portal of the Argo Tunnel would probably never encounter large amounts of high-grade ore that it could sell directly to the mint. The mill could probably produce some bullion, but virtually all the ore that the Argo Mill could buy would need to be upgraded before shipping to a smelter. With that knowledge, the mill designer needed to answer numerous questions.

Where were smelters located? How much would they pay for gold ore? How much would they pay for *concentrated* gold ore? How about silver? Were smelters willing to pay for other metals such as copper and lead? How much metal would smelters lose during refining? Did smelters impose penalties for certain kinds of contaminants? Did they pay premiums for specific types of ore or concentrates? Would they charge lower handling fees if material was crushed to a certain size?

The nearest smelters were in Denver, so a mill situated in Idaho Springs would need to ship material by rail. Thankfully, the Colorado & Southern Railroad (C&S) served Idaho Springs and its tracks passed less than 400 feet (122 m) from the mouth of the Argo Tunnel. Which smelters did the C&S serve? What were its shipping fees? What kinds of cars could the C&S provide? How much would each car hold? What were car sizes? How tall were the sides? Were cars made of wood or steel? Were there any weight restrictions going down Clear Creek Canyon? What extra fees would the C&S charge for switching cars to other railroads?

If a new mill were constructed at the Argo Tunnel, what were its main competitors and where were they located? How much did those mills pay? What were the reputations of those competitors? Did mills have "sweetheart deals" with particular mines or with the railroad? What kinds of processes did those mills use? Were there any new competitors on the horizon? Did mills buy ore or did they merely charge for processing? Did mills pay mines immediately or wait for weeks?

What mines were in operation at the time and what mills did they use? What was their ore like? Were mines likely to deliver ore by wagon, truck or rail? How dependable were mine reserves? How dependable were mine owners? How much ore were they likely to ship in a year? Could a new custom mill secure business by offering better prices?

Answers to questions like these would have guided the way the business was organized and what kinds of machinery it needed. Mine production was notoriously unreliable from week to week, so the Argo could not depend on consistent ore supplies from any single mine. The Argo mill would need to process ore from as many mines as possible over an area as wide as possible.

Argo Mill builders decided they could increase their competitiveness by buying ore directly from mines and paying immediately upon acceptance of offers. Management understood that most mine owners were too poor to survive long delays in payment.

The mill also decided to pay as much as possible for each ore's gold and silver content and would do so with a fixed price contract. The Argo wanted to pay miners almost as much as smelters did. The mill decided it would make its profit not on its purchase of ore, but upon processing fees. The Argo Mill would charge less than it would cost mines to maintain and operate their own dedicated mills.

Finally, mill designers knew ore supplies would be highly variable. Since they wanted the Argo Mill to last longer than normal mills, they built the Argo with steel instead of wood. To lower costs as much as possible, they aligned their various processes in a vertical manner. Every process used water, so a vertical orientation would help move ore downhill from process to process through pipes and minimize the need for uphill pumping.

On the verge of addressing the riddle of machinery, it is informative to review other knowledge Argo Mill designers had in 1912.

Core concepts

The richest ores in both Gilpin and Clear Creek counties had been removed years before. Not everything, of course. There were certainly rich pockets of "smelting ore" waiting to be found in some mines. However, occurrences of very rich ore would be rare.

Management decided the Argo needed to be a "reduction" mill. That meant that the mill would not try to produce a pure product. Instead it would reduce the volume of rock sent to smelters as much as possible. It would ship concentrates.

Gold mines are not separate from silver mines. In nature, it is rare to find either metal without the other. Ore from nearly everywhere in Gilpin and Clear Creek counties contained more silver than gold. However, because gold was so much more valuable, mines around Central City were generally considered to be gold mines. The ratio of silver to gold was usually higher in Clear Creek County, so that county held several silver districts.

During the initial operation of the Argo Mill, the United States maintained a stable price of gold fixed at $20.67 per troy ounce (66¢/g.) The price of silver varied with world demand but averaged about 71¢ per ounce (2.28¢/g.) Argo Mill processes were going to be optimized to capture as much gold as possible and that meant there would always be some silver loss.

Gold and silver deposits of Gilpin and Clear Creek counties are found associated with sulfide minerals contain copper, lead, zinc, and iron. Smelters would pay for those metals, but base metal prices were so low that it was not worth building in extra processes to try to recover them specifically.[63]

Economics changed with the outbreak of war in Europe and a consequent rise in the prices of copper and lead. Early in 1916, management shut down the mill for a few weeks so it could install new machinery in order to capture more of both base metals.

Business structure

The Argo Mill divided its business into three main functions:
- buying ore
- processing ore
- selling concentrates

The mill organized its business in a fashion so one function led naturally to the next. Each part of the business had to work closely with the others and each function required close monitoring. Inefficiency and breakdown in any one part of the business affected the entire enterprise.

Buying ore

Ore was the lifeblood of the mill. The Argo solicited ore from any mine that would sell. Every ore was different. Whether shipments were large or small, every delivery created several questions that needed answering before purchase:
- How much gold and silver was in the ore?
- How much would it cost to process that ore?
- What were competing mills paying for the same ore?
- How much would smelters pay for concentrates?
- How much could the mill afford to pay?
- Would mines accept the mill's purchase offers?

• Testing

The buying process started when ore shipments arrived at the mill, either from out of the tunnel or by rail or wagon from elsewhere. The mill first needed to learn how many tons were in the shipment and how much gold and silver was in each ton.

The west end of the mill was dedicated exclusively to sampling. Mill workers weighed entire shipments and stored each shipment in separate bins at tunnel level in the west end of the building. Shipments were then crushed and sub-divided several times to secure representative samples.

That resulting sample would have weighed a bit less than one percent of the entire shipment and would have been piled on the concrete floor of the *bucking room*[64] at ground level.

The large sample pile was then split in half several times until samplers ended up with a small, more manageable sample. *Splits* of the sample were given to the shipper, the mill, and the Argo's *assay* lab. The lab tested for metal content and reported final results in troy ounces per ton. Those values told the mill and the mines how much gold and silver was in each shipment.

- ***Purchase offer***

With those assay numbers, the mill calculated the total number of ounces of gold and silver in every inbound shipment. It then made offers that took into account milling costs and inevitable losses that the mill and smelter would incur. Unlike other mills, the Argo used a fixed price list. Every mine was treated equally.

If a mine accepted the mill's offer, a clerk wrote a check on the spot and the mill took possession of the shipment. At that time, workers moved crushed ore back to the top of the mill and dumped it into a large ore bin for processing sometime later.

It was inevitable that not all mines agreed with assay results. Existing records show that happened a few times during 1916 and a bit more frequently in 1917. In those cases, the Argo sent samples of reserved splits to another sampler in Idaho Springs for independent testing. Depending on the results of those second assays, mines decided to either accept or reject the Argo Mill's offers.

If mines thought Argo's offers were too low, they retrieved their entire shipments and sent them to competing mill elsewhere around Idaho Springs or Black Hawk. Records are unclear, but it appears a few mines took their ore elsewhere in 1917 and early 1918. Prices for silver, lead, and copper were high at that time, so other mills might have been paying more for those metals than the Argo. If so, one could question how those other mills made money.

- ***Ore supply***

The magnificent color and luster of gold shines on every aspect of the gold mining industry. It makes every aspect appear glamorous and rich.

In truth, it is expensive to produce gold. On average, profits tend to be surprisingly thin. Every step of the process, from exploration to numbering gold bars must be optimized to perfection. Cost efficiency is a never-ending quest. There is rarely room for waste anywhere along the line.

Once a mill is turned on, mill managers try to keep operations going continuously. The larger the mill, the more important it is to keep machinery in action. Starting and stopping mills is expensive. Costs are even higher in high-mountain climates where winters are long and idle machinery can freeze.

In old mining districts like those in Gilpin and Clear Creek counties, mines tended to be small. Few were able to ship ore continuously. Miners were always shifting operations from one area of a mine to another depending on conditions they encountered underground.

Production was never constant. Mines sometimes needed to stop production because of rock falls or because they needed to direct men to other tasks. It was not uncommon to stop mining operations because of labor shortages, weather, lack of supplies, machinery breakdowns, and water. Water was always a concern. Interruptions tended to be surprises.

Ore shipments to the Argo Mill were always unpredictable. The Argo had built a large 1,600-ton (1,451 tonne) ore bin at the top of the mill to help it keep working during slack times and avoid over-time costs during busy times. With an initial processing capability of 120 tons (109 tonnes) per day,[65] the Argo had the flexibility to work for at least 16 days, even if ore shipments had stopped completely.

Processing ore

A mill is very much like a house of magic. It is all about tricks. Tricking rock to let go of gold. Tricking gold to go one way while sending rock another. Tricking gold into floating when it really wants to sink.

Some tricks were relatively new when the Argo Mill started up; some were centuries old. Some tricks worked better than others and all worked best under specific conditions. Regardless of near-magical methods, milling is all about removing rock and keeping gold.

- *Grasping the scale of the problem*

To truly grasp the magic, one needs to appreciate the scale of the problem. It is important to realize that gold was rarely visible to the naked eye in the ore that came to Argo Mill. Most gold particles were microscopic.

Based on real results, the Argo Mill mathematically processed 3,850 pounds (1,746 kg) of ore to recover one troy ounce of gold during its first five years of operation. Stating the mill's effort like that, however, radically understates the problem. Let's look at the mill from a *particle* perspective.

If the mill crushed 3,850 pounds of ore to a uniform, average-sized grain of sand, it would have a pile of 45,000,000,000 (45 billion) grains to sort through. Within that amount, there would be one grain of pure gold for every 394,000 grains of rock. That would be the equivalent of searching for one specific person among five and a half NFL football stadiums packed to capacity.

Particles, of course, were neither uniform in size nor identical in character. It is hard to fathom such monstrous numbers, but the Argo Mill had the capacity to process several *trillion* particles in an average day.

- *Crushing*

No process can grab gold particles effectively until they are released from the rock that holds them. That is where crushing comes in.

It seems logical that the more finely ore is crushed, the more gold would be liberated. However, the more finely ore is crushed, the more rock particles there are to process. More particles means more searching. And more losses. Mills always face a form of the Goldilocks conundrum; particle sizes should be neither too coarse nor too fine.

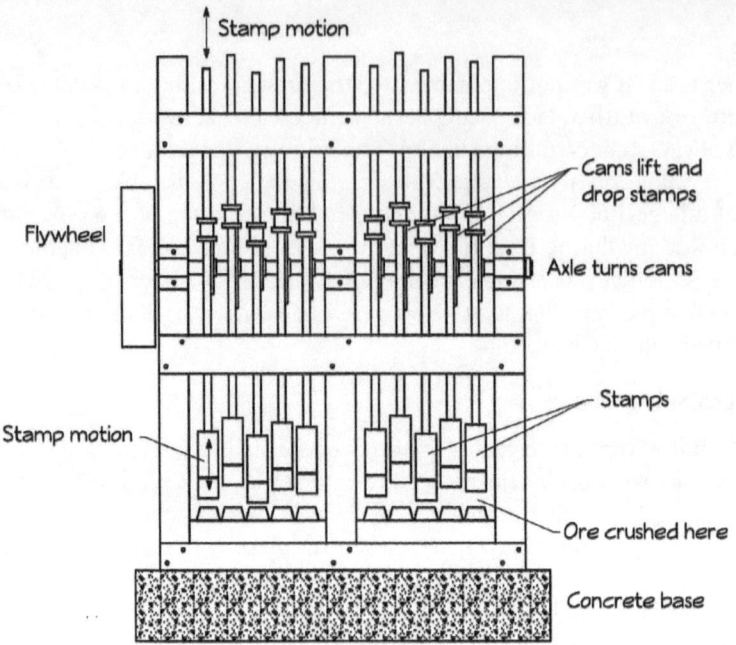

Stamp Mill

The first step in most mills, including the Argo, was to crush ore in a stamp mill. This illustration shows 10 heavy pistons or "stamps." The Argo Mill used 20 stamps, 10 of which crushed ore slightly finer than the others. The stamps reduced ore to particles that, if placed on a table, would be no taller than the thickness of about 11 leaves in this book. That is the *maximum* size; most was smaller.

Upon arrival at the Argo Mill, every ore shipment was crushed to the size of gravel. That size was small enough for sampling purposes, but was much too large for extracting gold. The mill needed to crush ore much finer before processing.

At the time the Argo Mill was built, *stamp mills* were the most efficient crushing method. Other kinds of crushers were available, but they did not have the capacity needed to process 120 tons of ore every day.

Stamp mills were simple assemblages of heavy pistons mounted on steel rods. The pistons were known as *stamps* and were mounted side by side in a frame, much like pistons in an automobile engine. Conveyors fed ore into the stamps while belt-driven cams lifted and dropped the stamps in succession. The stamps created a wet, gritty slurry of crushed rock that ranged from the size of ordinary sand down to the size of table salt. Inevitably, some amount of rock was pulverized into powder.

Mill operators had argued for years whether it was better to crush ore by dropping light-weight stamps from a greater height or heavy stamps from a shorter distance. The Argo chose the latter approach and installed four batteries of stamps with five heavy stamps per battery.

Each stamp weighed 1,050 pounds (476 kg.). Cams mounted on heavy steel axles lifted stamps about six inches (15 cm.) It took two to three seconds to raise and drop a single stamp, but with all five stamps working together, a stamp battery created 100 to 144 impacts every minute.[66] If more than one battery were in use, the mill would have created a steady and loud bang-bang-bang at roughly the rate of a typical pocket watch.

Once crushed to a desired size, ore flowed down through each level of the building where subsequent processes removed more and more worthless rock.

Argo Mill processes

The Argo Mill used five main technologies over its lifespan:
- amalgamation
- sizing
- separation using gravity
- cyanidation
- froth flotation

The mill opened for business around April 1, 1913.[67] Within months, owners realized that the mill was losing too much gold. Owners replaced the original mill manager by November and his replacement made changes to processes and plant layout before the end of the year.[68] Management revamped the mill again in February, 1916 and engineering literature reported further renovations at the mill in 1921. The Colorado Bureau of Mines, however, failed to further mention the mill until 1934 and then nothing after 1935. Following are abbreviated discussions of each major process. It is important to realize that mill managers constantly adjusted machinery and processes. They tended to be obsessive about trying to save another dime. Constant experimentation and adjustment was the rule. Managers changed the mill several times, so discussions of the Argo Mill in professional journals were always snapshots in time.

- *Amalgamation*

One of the most curious qualities of gold, silver, copper, and a few other metals is their ability to alloy with mercury at room temperature. This fascinating process is called amalgamation. When gold touches mercury, it melts or dissolves into the mercury, creating a viscous, putty-like alloy called *amalgam* (uh-MAL-gum).

Amalgamation tables were part of the original Argo Mill design. The tables were nothing more than sheets of copper nailed to wooden decks, three or four feet wide, and tipped at slight angles. Mercury was poured over the copper sheets and workers smeared the mercury around until it coated the sheets from top to bottom and edge to edge. Conceptually, mercury would stick to copper and then gold would stick to mercury.

Amalgamation tables were placed immediately below the stamp mills. Crushed ore flowed out of the stamps and down the amalgamation tables before moving on to other processes. Rock particles passed over the mercury with no effect, but gold and silver particles stuck to mercury with stunning effectiveness.

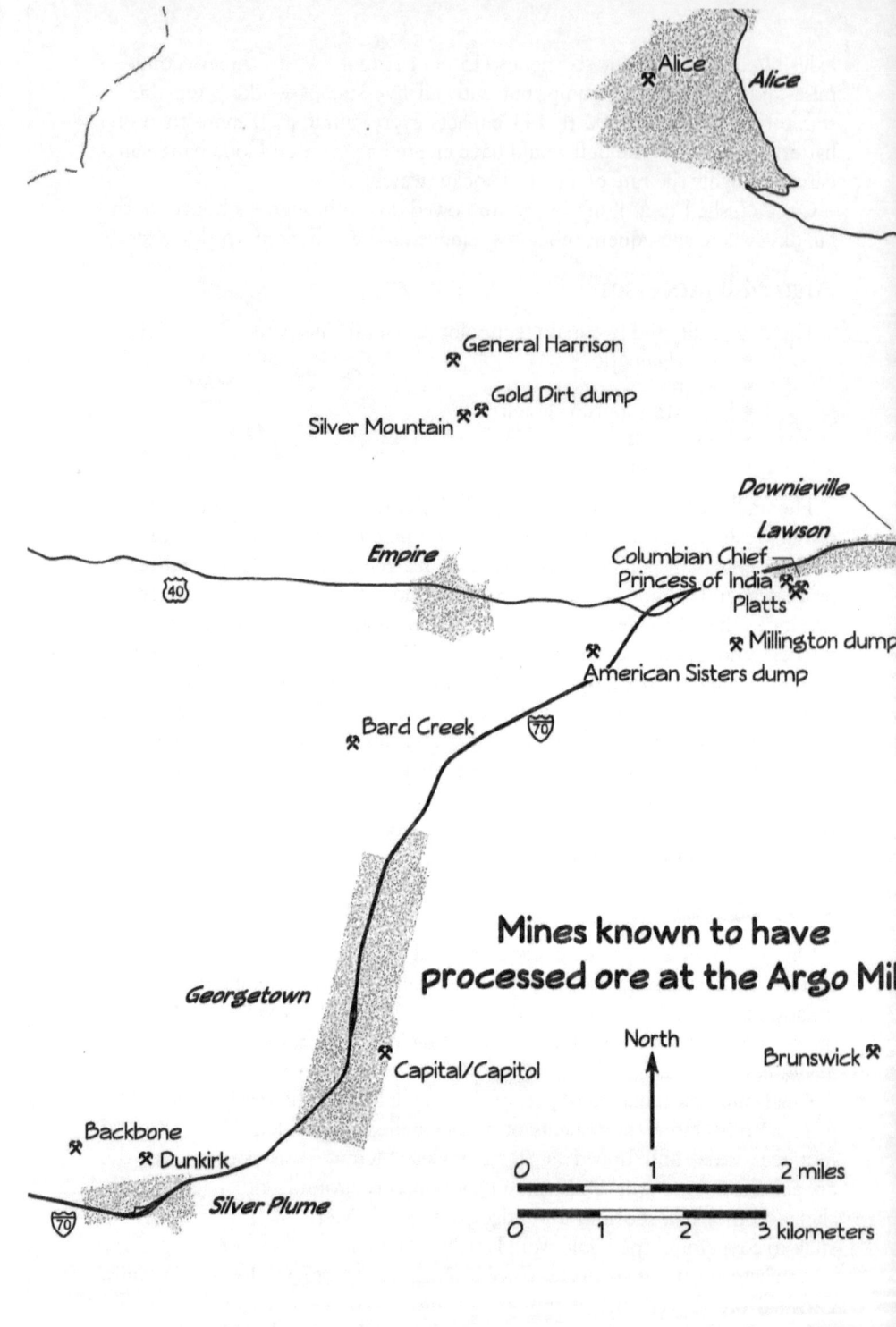

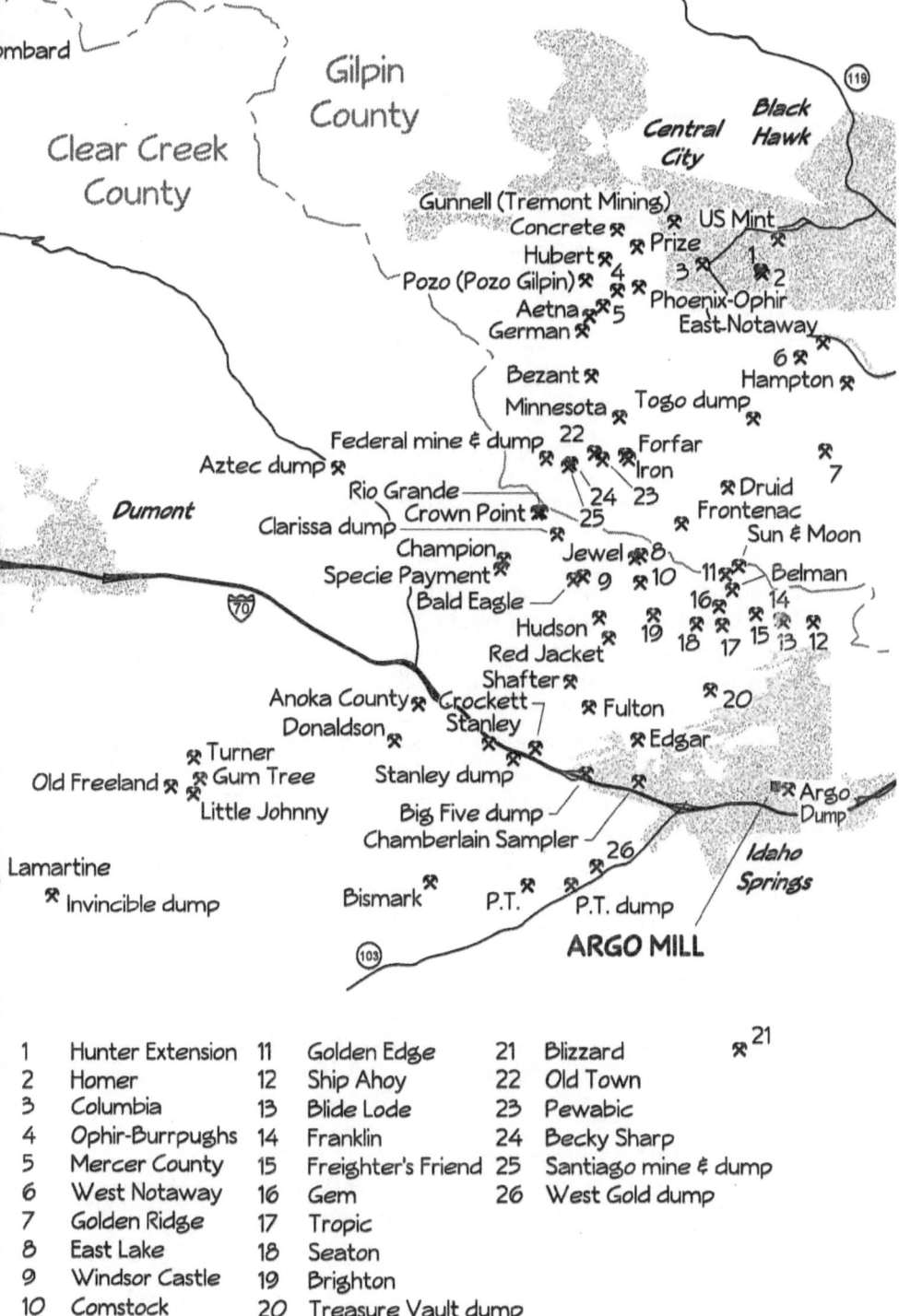

1	Hunter Extension	11	Golden Edge	21	Blizzard	
2	Homer	12	Ship Ahoy	22	Old Town	
3	Columbia	13	Blide Lode	23	Pewabic	
4	Ophir-Burrpughs	14	Franklin	24	Becky Sharp	
5	Mercer County	15	Freighter's Friend	25	Santiago mine & dump	
6	West Notaway	16	Gem	26	West Gold dump	
7	Golden Ridge	17	Tropic			
8	East Lake	18	Seaton			
9	Windsor Castle	19	Brighton			
10	Comstock	20	Treasure Vault dump			

These are *some* of the mines known to have sold ore to the Argo Mill. Not all mines were identifiable because the mill sometimes recorded purchases the names of persons and companies that delivered ore, not the originating mines.

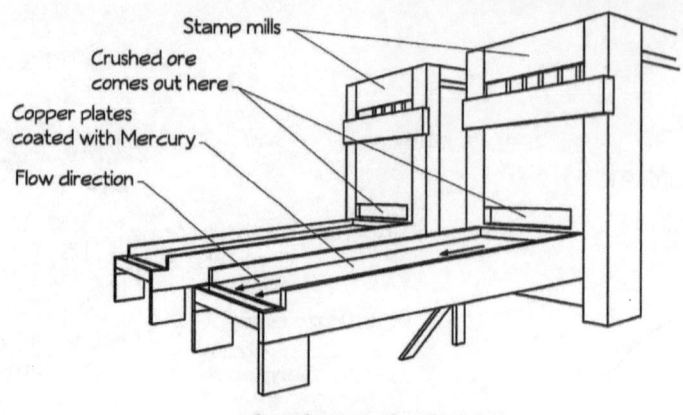

Amalgamation Tables
Typically situated immediately below stamp mills

Like almost all mills in the area, the Argo Mill was initially used amalgamation tables. The mill mostly abandoned their use by 1914. because the tables had proven largely ineffective for the sulfide-rich ores the Argo Mill was processing.

In an industrial setting like the Argo, workers would have constantly balanced and the amounts of crushed ore and water in an effort to minimize gold loss. As more and more gold and silver alloyed with the mercury, the mercury turned from a shiny silver to a dull gray. The grayer the mercury, the less effective it was at capturing gold.

When the mercury became dull, workers would stop the flow of ore and scrape amalgam from the copper with pieces of wood or hard rubber. They would transfer the amalgam to iron containers (mercury does not stick to iron), add fresh coats of mercury to the copper, and restart the flow of ore.

Once they accumulated a sufficient quantity, workers would squeeze globs of amalgam through fine cloths or chamois to remove excess mercury. Left behind would have been many pounds of very heavy, dull gray amalgam containing high percentages of gold.

The next step was to separate the gold from the mercury through a method called *retorting*. Amalgam was heated in covered iron *retorts* to a temperature at which mercury evaporated. The process was a closed system, so the mercury gas was captured, cooled, and condensed back into liquid form for re-use.

WARNING. WARNING. WARNING. Many miners in the early days of Colorado gold mining died while heating amalgam to drive off mercury. Mercury gas is highly toxic and exceedingly dangerous. Readers are expressly warned against the practice.

After the mercury was driven off and re-constituted in liquid form, a porous, sponge-like mass of gold and silver called *doré* (pronounced door-RAY) remained. Workers then melted the doré and poured the gold-silver alloy into bars. The mill then shipped the bars to the U. S. Mint at Denver for payment.

Mill configuration 1
April, 1913 to November, 1913

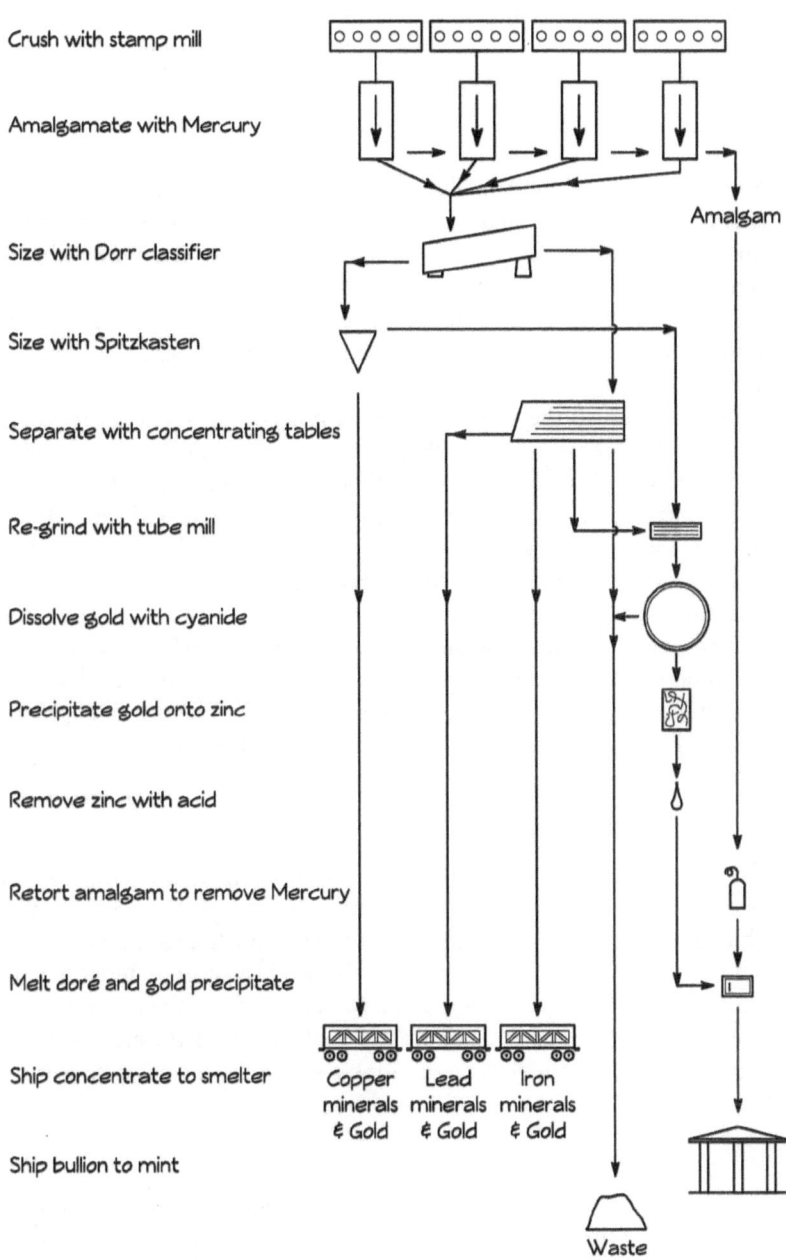

Diagram of the way ore flowed move through the Argo Mill during the first six months of operation.

The Argo Mill used amalgamation in its initial 1913 design, but operators were already talking about abandoning the process within months.[69] They complained that sulfide-rich ores scoured copper plates badly and washed away much of the accumulated amalgam. After 1913, technical literature barely mentioned amalgamation in relation to the Argo Mill. It appears that the mill may not have abandoned the process entirely, but might have used it sparingly on certain kinds of ores.

- *Sizing*

Processes downstream from the stamp mills recovered gold in ways quite different than age-old amalgamation. All processes, however, shared one common feature: the more uniform the particle size, the better the gold recovery.

The concept is somewhat like coin sorters seen in banks. In order to determine values of bags of coins, coins are first sorted by size. Counting then becomes easy.

A mill works much the same way, just with billions of small particles. After sorting, sand-sized particles would be sent through one process and grit through another. There would be another process to handle ultra-fine dust. Each size might have held gold, but methods for getting to gold varied by size.

In a gold mill, processes are designed to deal with particles in narrow ranges of sizes. Separating material by size is called *classification* and the machines that do the work are called *classifiers*.

A large amount of material must flow through a gold mill every minute. Speed is important and time is money. It is very easy to separate large sizes, but the smaller the particle size, the slower and harder the task. Mill processes would work extremely well if ore were classified perfectly, but that never happens in real life.

— *Sieve screens*

The Argo Mill used three main classification methods. The first were screens located in the bottom compartments of stamp mills. Stamps would crush chunks of ore into pieces, some tiny, some much larger. Small material would flow out through holes in the screens, while coarser material remained in the mill to be hit by the stamps again. Material shrunk progressively smaller in size with every hit and material that finally escaped through stamp mill screens were a bit smaller than coarse table salt. Subsequent sizing was more precise, but only to a point.

— *Rake classifiers*

The Argo Mill used several rake classifiers made by a company named "Dorr." These weird-looking devices were large rectangular bins filled with water. Each classifier had a bottom that sloped steeply from one end to the other. Gold-bearing sands were fed into the classifier near the deep end while a series of wooden rakes pulled the sand-like material along the bottom

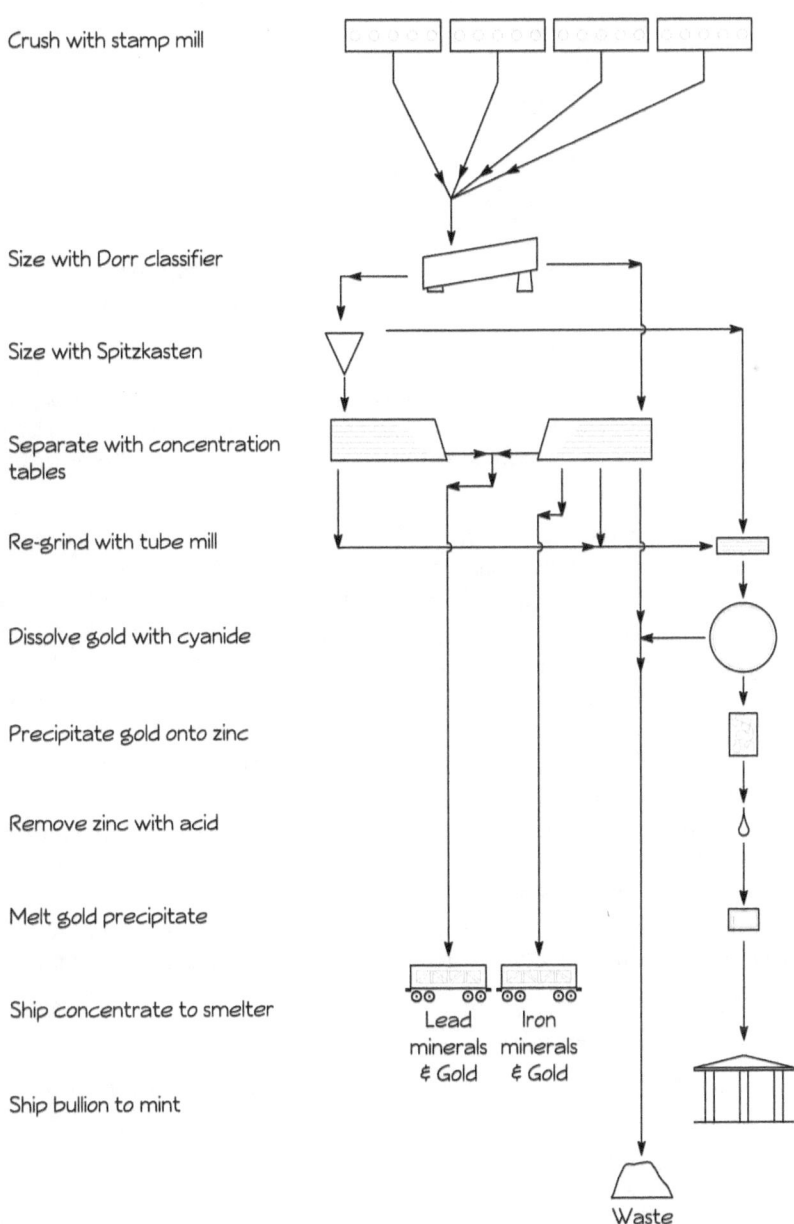

Mill configuration 2
November, 1913 to February, 1916

Crush with stamp mill

Size with Dorr classifier

Size with Spitzkasten

Separate with concentration tables

Re-grind with tube mill

Dissolve gold with cyanide

Precipitate gold onto zinc

Remove zinc with acid

Melt gold precipitate

Ship concentrate to smelter

Ship bullion to mint

Lead minerals & Gold

Iron minerals & Gold

Waste

Operators quickly realized amalgamation in the first mill configuration was working poorly with the types of ores being run through the mill. This second configuration was very similar to the first, shows that the effort to separately recover copper sulfides for refining had been an unnecessary extra step.

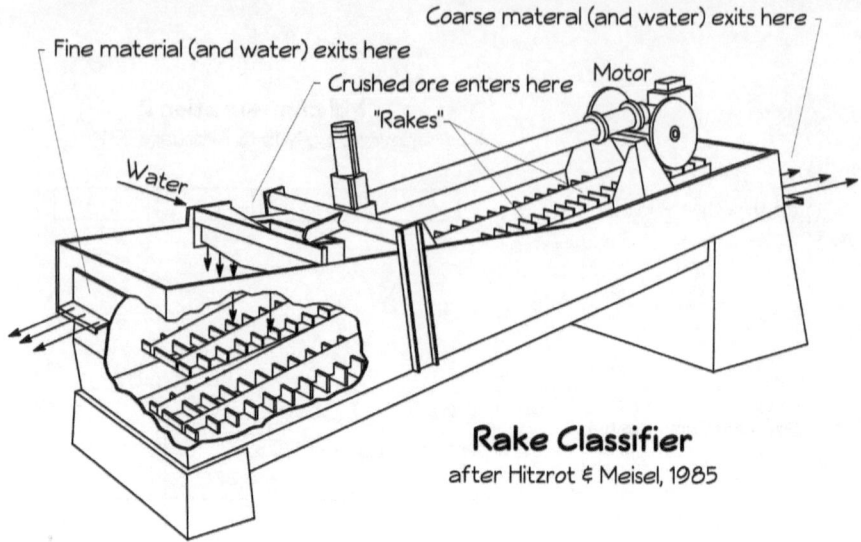

Rake Classifier
after Hitzrot & Meisel, 1985

This odd-looking device "classified" or separated particles of ore by size. Most were built by the Dorr company and some can still be seen in the Argo Mill. Coarse material, removed at the right side, was sent to Wilfley tables for further separation by density.

upslope toward the shallow end. (The rakes were not like the fingers of ordinary garden rakes, but simply flat pieces of lumber.)

The rakes did not touch the bottom of the bin, but merely pulled small piles of sandy material toward the upper end of the bin like a conveyor belt. As the rakes moved upward, they created eddies and currents that lifted the finer material. Small and lighter particles tended to flow over the upward moving rakes while the coarser material stayed near the bottom of the bin and progressed further upward and ultimately out of the machine. Fine material flowed out the opposite end.

The process of sizing material in such manner sounds haphazard and inefficient, but rake classifiers did an oddly good job of separating coarse sizes from *fines*. The goal was not to capture gold, but merely sort coarser particles from finer particles. Depending on the next process in the mill, ore might have moved through one or more Dorr classifiers, each adjusted a bit differently.

— *Cone classifier*

The earliest mill designs indicate that the Argo mill pumped finer material from rake classifiers into a cone classifier to make a second size separation. The particular device used at the Argo was called a Spitzkasten.

Crushed ore was fed into a rectangular-shaped cone. Gritty particles wanted to sink to the bottom of the cone but were lifted by a stream of water coming up from the bottom. Only the coarsest and heaviest particles ever reached the bottom; everything lighter flowed out of the top. Coarse material flowed out of a pipe near the bottom and into a subsequent process while lighter material moved to another.

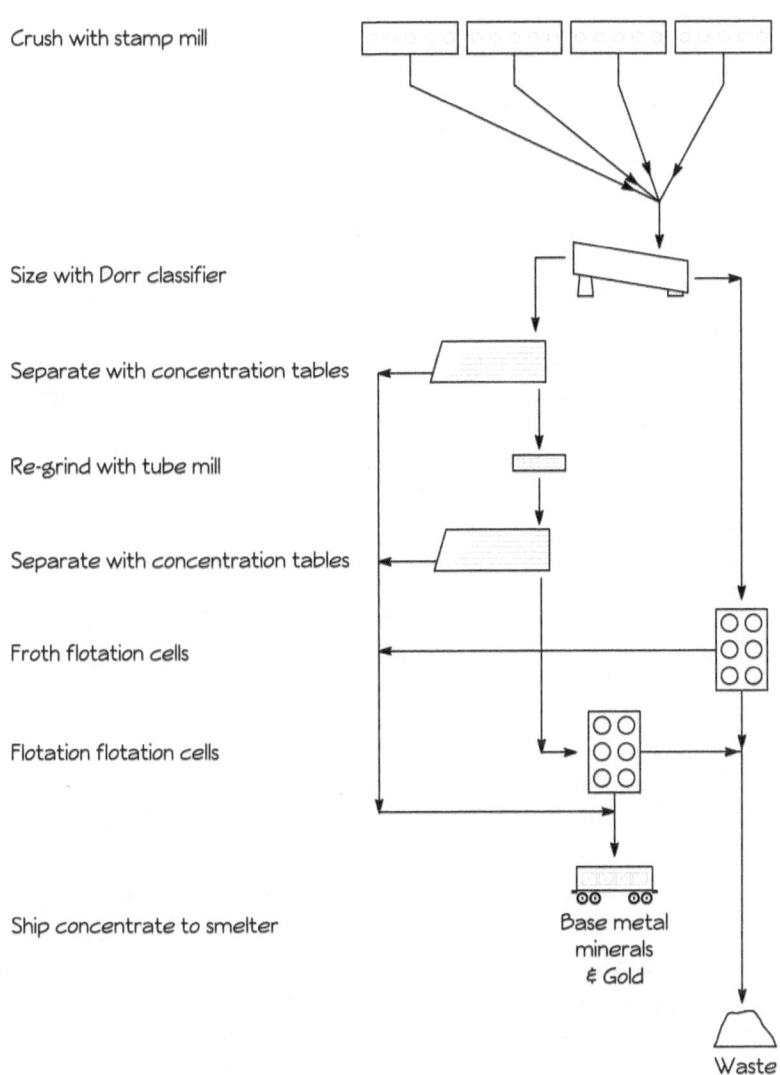

Mill configuration 3
February, 1916 to April, 1919

Crush with stamp mill

Size with Dorr classifier

Separate with concentration tables

Re-grind with tube mill

Separate with concentration tables

Froth flotation cells

Flotation flotation cells

Ship concentrate to smelter

Base metal minerals & Gold

Waste

Third version of processes within the Argo Mill used until the mill closed down after World War I. Note that after removing cyanide from the circuit, the mill had abandoned its effort to capture gold and silver for sale to the mint, in favor of a heavier reliance on smelters to capture maximum metal values. No reliable information exists about mill operations or equipment used in later years, but it seems likely that later owners may have re-introduced older techniques because all nearby smelters had closed.

Some mills made several size classifications by adding two or more cones downstream from the first, each one larger than the one before. Technical literature indicates that the Argo used a Spitzkasten until 1916, but it is unclear whether it used a single cone or multiples.

- *Gravity separation*

Whereas classifiers separated particles based primarily on size, other devices made separations based on density. Like amalgamation, gravity separation is an ancient technique, possibly the oldest. The trick relies on the great density of gold compared to ordinary rock.

Most people have a passing familiarity with gold panning. Machines in the Argo Mill used gravity much in the same way. The basic idea was to wash away light material with water and leave dense gold behind.

With brief instruction, practically anyone can learn how to recover gold with a gold pan. Panning can be done with dry material, but it works tremendously better with water. Plain old water is the trick.

Admittedly, mills don't use gold pans, but nonetheless separate gold from rock using the same principle.

Understanding the behaviors of gold and rock is easier if we enlarge tiny particles to something more life-size. The size of a golf ball is universal, so works well as an example.

If a golf ball were made out of gold, it would weigh 25.2 troy ounces, the equivalent of about 1.7 U.S. pounds or 0.8 kilograms.

By comparison, a golf ball made out of typical rock found in the area of the Argo Mill would weigh only 3.6 troy ounces. Regardless of whether we're talking about golf balls or sand size particles, gold is seven times heavier in *air* than rock. Big surprise.

But...just like a human body feels much lighter in water, so does gold and rock. This table shows how much the gold and rock golf balls would weigh in both air and water. The rightmost column shows that gold is *over ten times(!) heavier* than ordinary rock when measured in water.

Weights of gold and rock "golf balls" in troy ounces (grams)

	Gold	Rock	Ratio
Weight in air	25.2 (784)	3.6 (112)	25.2 ÷ 3.6 = 7.0
Weight in water	23.9 (743)	2.3 (72)	23.9 ÷ 2.3 = 10.3

That is why gold panning works so much better with water than air!

In the technical jargon of a gold mill, a gold pan would be described as a simple but highly effective "gravity separation device."

The Argo and other mills depended heavily on gravity separation devices to wash away worthless rock from gold and other heavy materials using water combined with vibration, shaking, and agitation.

— Concentration tables

Like most gold mills built in the region, the Argo depended heavily on *concentration tables*. These devices are very simple, highly effective, non-toxic, and still used all over the world to capture both precious and non-precious metals.

Typically, concentration tables are rectangular, longer in one direction and tilted from one corner to the opposite corner. They are connected to the axle of an electric motor to make them shake back and forth in the long direction and often called shaker tables. Sized gold ore and a light stream of water is fed onto the table near the highest corner as the table is shaking.

Smooth tables would not accomplish anything. Instead, long, narrow wooden strips are nailed to tables parallel to long edges and spaced two or more inches apart. The strips are planed so they are about a quarter inch high at one end and taper gradually down to nothing toward the downstream end of the table.

By adjusting water flow, tilt and shaking, lighter sand washes over the wooden strips and eventually off the long edge of the table. It mimics the way prospectors wash away light sand from the lips of gold pans. And like the way gold remains in the bottoms of gold pans, dense minerals and gold remain behind the wooden strips. The jostling action of the table gradually moves gold and other dense particles down the strips until they fall off the narrow end of the table.

JASON AND THE GOLDEN FLEECE

The word "Argo" comes from an ancient Greek story in which King Pelias sent Jason on a quest to recover a golden fleece from a mythical winged ram. In his adventures, Jason sailed around the Aegean and Black Seas in a ship named *Argo*. His crewmen were named *Argonauts*.

Argo remains a popular name in U.S. gold mining. Many mines in the American West were named Argo, including one in Russell Gulch, north of Idaho Springs, one along Chicago Creek south of town, and a third near Empire. Three *Golden Fleece* claims are also known in Gilpin and Clear Creek Counties. Many gold mining districts throughout the West have at least one claim named Argo or Golden Fleece. That brings up a question:

What was so special about fleece in 8th century BC Greece?

It was common in ancient times to place fleece, the skin and soft wooly hair of sheep, in the bottoms of sluices to capture fine particles of gold. One of the odd qualities of gold is that it has a strong affinity for oil and grease. Fleece is particularly effective at capturing gold because the hair is covered with lanolin, a wax secreted by sebaceous glands in the skin of sheep.

The attraction of gold to lanolin was also used to recover gold in desert areas where sand dunes formed from gold-bearing rocks. Sand from the lower levels of dunes was shoveled onto fleece and shaken by two people. Gold settled deep into the fleece fibers and was held there by the lanolin. Gold was then recovered by washing or burning the fleece.

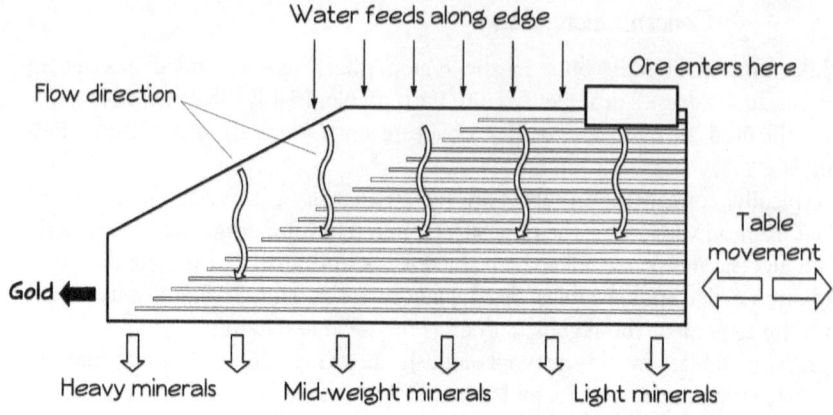

Concentration Table

Arthur Wilfley invented concentration tables (aka Wilfley table or shaker table) in 1896. They were widely adopted in many mills shortly thereafter because they were so effective at classifying (concentrating) gold and heavy minerals by density. Derivatives of his designs are still in constant use around the globe.

Concentration tables have the remarkable ability to separate high-value heavy material from lower-value, lighter material. *Lower value* does not necessarily mean *no value*. At the Argo Mill, lighter material was usually sent from concentration tables to other processes for further treatment.

- *Cyanidation*

Neither oxidation, corrosion, nor any single acid will affect gold. Prior to 1783, only two liquids were known to dissolve gold: mercury and *Aqua regia*. Aqua regia is a very nasty, dangerous mixture of concentrated hydrochloric acid and nitric acid.

A Swedish chemist discovered in 1783 that a solution of sodium cyanide would also dissolve gold, especially if the gold particles were small. It took until about 1890 for metallurgists to adopt the concept of using cyanide to extract gold on a scale conducive to commercial gold mining.

The Argo Mill used cyanide to capture gold in a method called *vat leaching*. Small-sized gold ore was submerged in large tanks filled with a sodium cyanide solution. After soaking for a certain period of time, the cyanide/gold solution was removed from the vats and sent to still another process to separate gold from the cyanide. Spent ore left in the bottom of the vat was essentially devoid of gold. It was then washed and neutralized to remove any remaining cyanide and discarded.

Once collected, the loaded–or *pregnant*–cyanide solution with its dissolved precious metals could be treated in a variety of ways. The Argo Mill directed its pregnant cyanide solution through boxes filled with zinc shavings. Gold precipitated onto the zinc and the zinc was dissolved away with acid. The gold and silver was then melted and poured into bars.

Today, cyanidation is responsible for recovering the majority of new gold produced by mining. That does not mean it is without its problems.

Spy movies created during the Cold War taught the public that hydrogen cyanide is a deadly poison when consumed, breathed, or contacted. While sodium cyanide is much more controllable in industrial settings, threats of injury and death remain. Considering the wide use of cyanidation, it was inevitable that some disasters would happen and will probably happen again. No evidence has emerged to suggest there were any injuries or incidences at the Argo Mill due to cyanide poisoning.

Cyanidation at the Argo Mill was effective at dissolving gold and silver from crushed ore. However, a certain amount of silver was lost during the precipitation onto zinc. Moreover a certain amount of both gold and silver was tied up in sulfides that cyanidation did not treat with great effectiveness. Significant silver was tied up in a lead sulfide called *galena* (pronounced "guh-LEEN-uh.") If properly tuned, gravity separation could be used to capture galena, but galena was not initially a target for processing when the mill was built. Silver prices were low , so the loss of some silver was not initially concerning.

Once war broke out in Europe, demand for base metals like lead and copper rose sharply. Prices for lead rose about 20% and copper showed a 30% gain. Neither metal was ever going to be a significant profit center for the Argo Mill, but because lead and copper sulfides were so common, the value of base metals sometimes ores exceeded silver values. Why not try to capture lead, copper, and silver and decrease some of the losses sustained through cyanidation?

- **Froth Flotation**

Management had known about the technology of flotation but did not include it in the original 1913 Argo Mill design. By 1915, the use of flotation in the mining industry had grown substantially and held more promise than initially thought. Management studied its alternatives during late 1915 and eventually closed the mill for two weeks in January, 1916. During that shutdown, engineers made huge changes to the mill's process flows. They increased reliance on gravity separation and added froth flotation,[70] in an effort to capture more copper and lead.[71] Management decreased the use of cyanidation while studying results and costs of the floatation technology. Shortly thereafter, management abandoned the cyanide process completely, although it is unclear whether engineers removed all its cyanide equipment or merely repurposed some of it.

Like other aspects of milling, froth flotation[72] is yet another way of tricking gold to move away from rock. It takes advantage of another peculiarity of nature, in particular, the odd behavior of gold, oil and grease.

In the presence of water, minerals with shiny *metallic luster* stick to fats and oils, while ordinary rock dust, sands, and earthy minerals do not. There was ancient knowledge of the phenomenon (see sidebar on Jason and the Golden

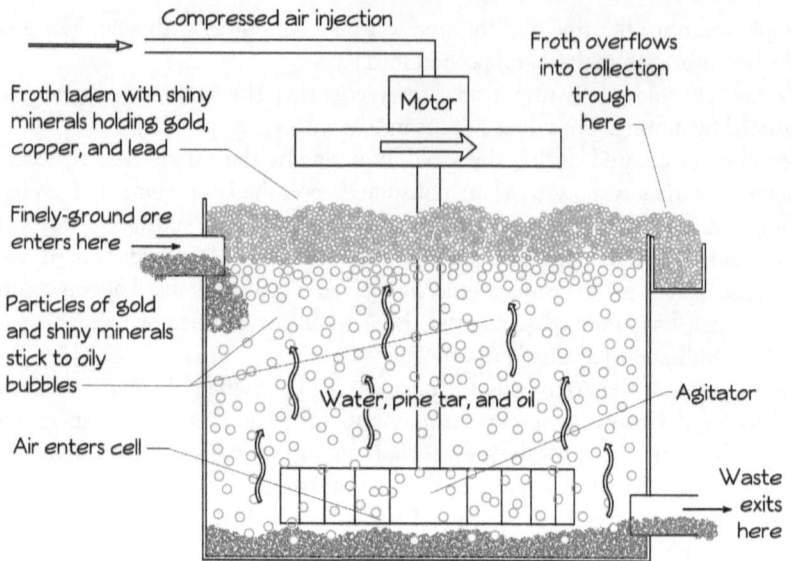

Froth Flotation Cell

As prices for lead and copper rose, cyanide became somewhat of a liability. Froth flotation was better at capturing very fine particles of silver, gold, and copper while the concentration tables were good at capturing larger particles of gold, silver, and lead. (Note how the mill configuration changed between #2 and #3.)

Fleece), but it took until 1877 for two German brothers to develop a commercial process for separating a lustrous type of graphite from ordinary rock. The first American patent for flotation process was awarded in 1886, and subsequently tested on sulfide-rich ores at Georgetown, Colorado and other places around 1890.

Inventors sensed the tremendous potential of flotation, so experimentation blossomed worldwide, setting off the filing of competing patents and years of litigations. The Argo Mill avoided the courts by developing its own twist on the flotation process.

The process worked by submerging crushed ore in a tank filled with a mixture of water, petroleum oil, and a light pine tar. Large amounts of air were pumped into the bottom of the tank, creating vigorous agitation and millions

HOW MUCH DOES A "TYPICAL" GOLD BAR WEIGH?

Gold bars are sold in a wide variety of sizes and weights, but the sizes most frequently portrayed in movies are 400 troy ounce "Good Delivery" bars like stored in Fort Knox, Kentucky.

Weight of a typical Good Delivery bar
400 troy ounces = 27.4 pounds = 12.4 kilograms

of bubbles. Lustrous minerals such as galena, chalcopyrite (a copper-iron mineral), silver, and gold stuck to the bubbles and floated to the surface. As the froth of bubbles grew, the oily bubbles with their attached minerals floated over the edge of the tank into a collection trough. Although particles of worthless rock were lighter than gold and lead, they repelled oil and sank to the bottom.

Once the Argo Mill began using froth flotation, it was able to recover and pay mines for copper. It also increased its ability to recover lead. By paying for those two base metals, the Argo Mill helped make every client mine a bit more profitable. Between early 1916 and the end of 1918, the mill sent over 717 tons of lead and 240 tons of copper to smelters.

OFFICIAL UNITED STATES GOLD PRICES

Dollars per troy ounce	As of:	Event
$19.39	Apr. 2, 1792	Mint Act
$20.69	Jun. 28, 1834	Devaluation Act of 1834
$20.67	Feb. 12, 1873	Coinage Act of 1873
	Jun. 5, 1933	Gold standard suspended
$20.67	Jan. 30, 1934	Gold Reserve Act
$35.00	Jan 31, 1934	Presidential Proclamation 2072
$38.00	Dec. 18, 1971	Smithsonian Agreement
$42.22	Sep. 21, 1973	Public Law 93-110
	Oct. 19, 1976	Gold standard removed

Beware: Online sources do not accurately quote the value of gold at various times in American history, particularly between 1834 and 1873. It is often necessary to consult enabling legislation and convert from specified grains of gold at specific fineness to derive dependable values in troy ounces.

Selling concentrate

The Argo Mill bought ore from mines and once miners accepted Argo's offers and paid, the mill owned the ore. The amount Argo paid took into account how much it would receive upon sale of gold, silver, lead, and copper as well as all the various costs of crushing, milling, and shipping concentrates.

Miners probably never fully enjoyed the amounts the Argo Mill was willing to pay for their ore. Nor is there any indication they fully appreciated that the large Argo Mill offered economies of scale that the miners' own mills could never have achieved.

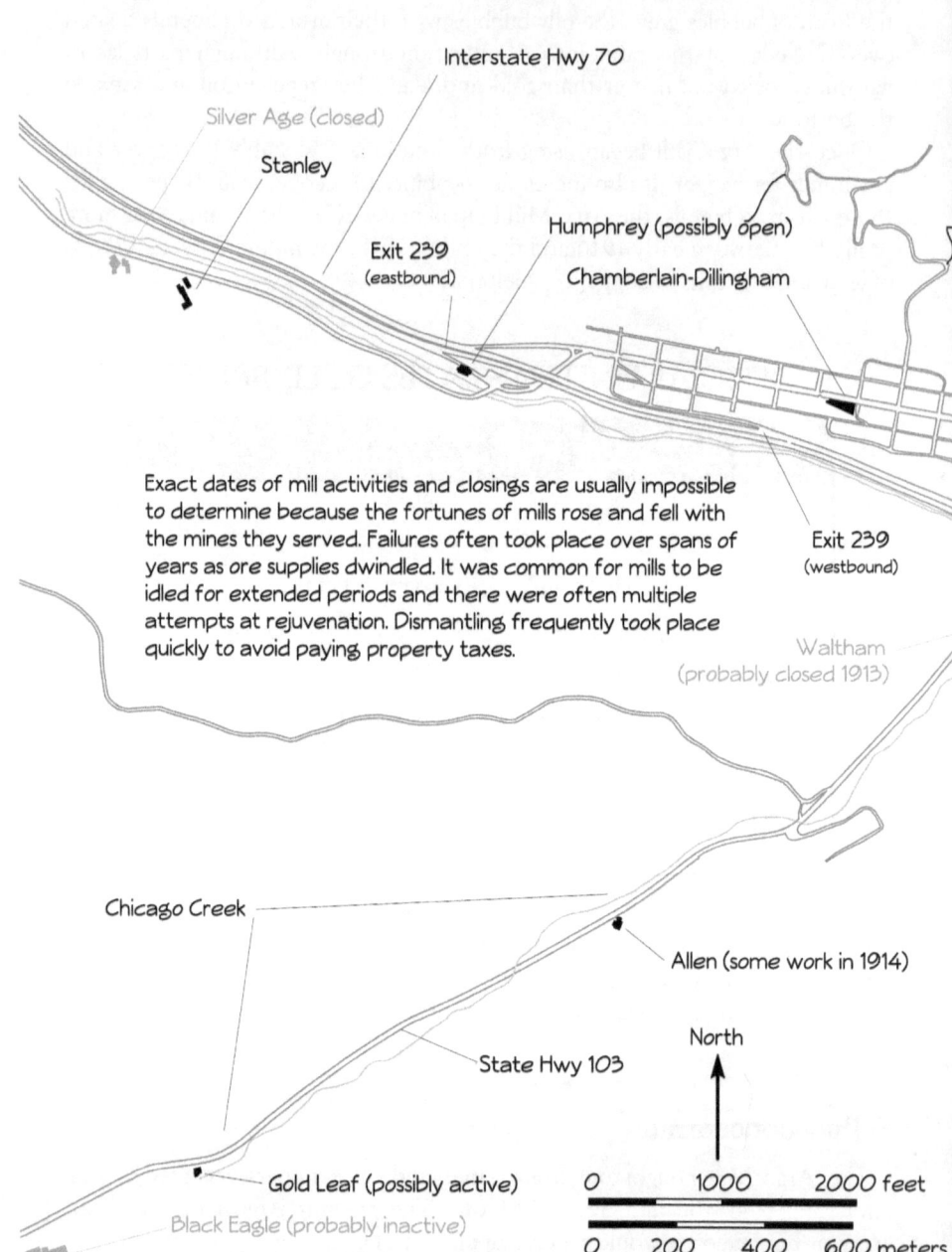

The Argo Mill was designed and built as a "custom mill" to buy and process ore from many different mines, all with somewhat different ores. Numerous other custom mills in the vicinity could have been competitors, but most had closed before the Argo became operational in 1913. The Argo, therefore, helped keep several mines open during World War I that might otherwise have failed.

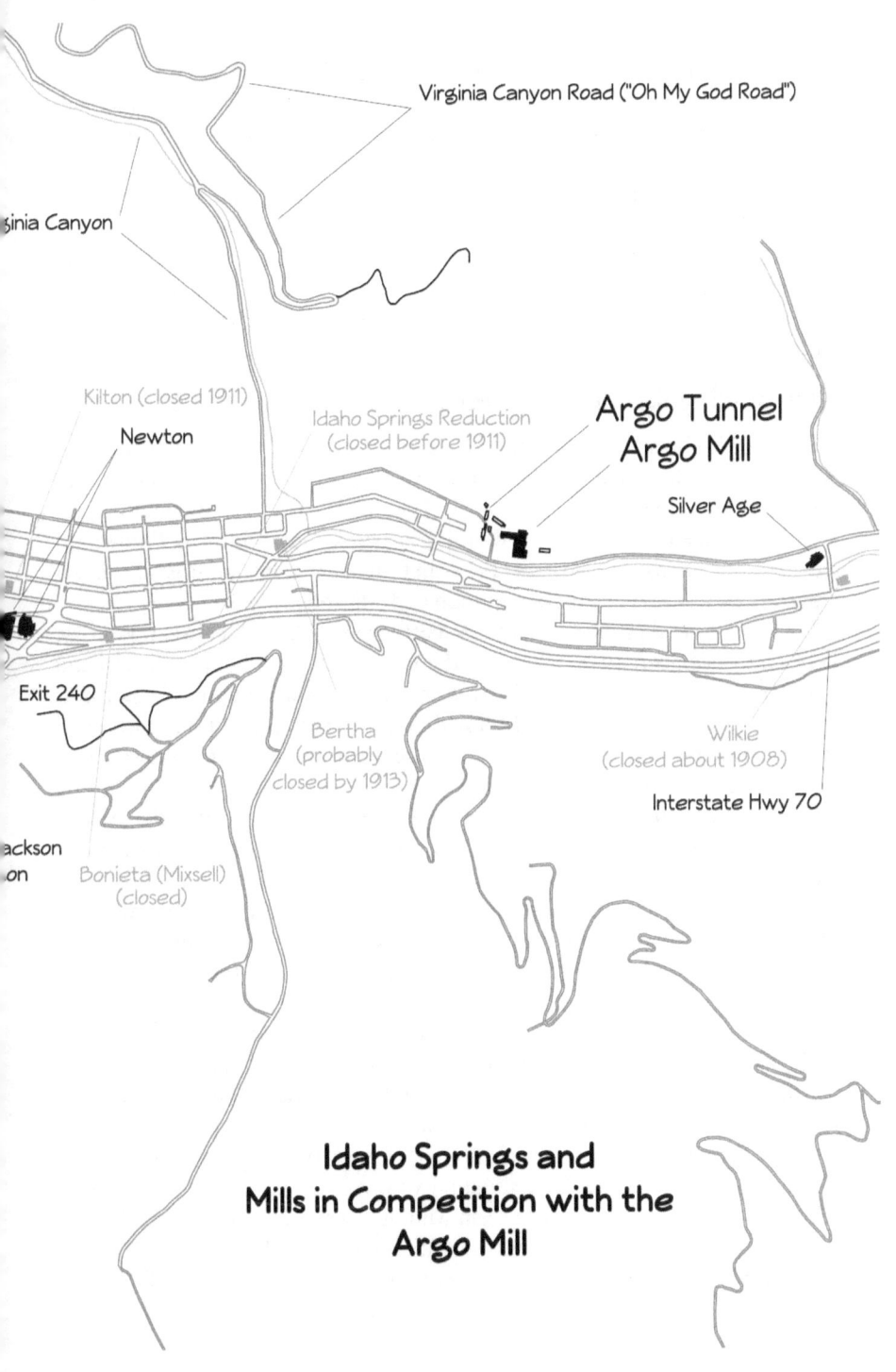

The Argo shipped most of its concentrates to the American Smelting and Refining Company (ASARCO) smelter in Denver. Occasionally, the mill shipped some of its concentrate to the Modern Smelter at Golden and a different ASARCO smelter in Omaha, Nebraska. In 1920, ASARCO converted its Denver smelter to an arsenic refinery and forced local ores to be shipped all the way to an ASARCO smelter in Leadville.

Back in 1909, before the tunnel had reached its final length, Samuel Newhouse had proposed building a smelter near the tunnel and mill site. Only the slightest mention of the proposal ever got into print and the idea never got off the ground.

How much gold and silver did the Argo Mill produce?

Samuel Newhouse had originally conceived of a mill at the mouth of the Argo Tunnel, but had moved onto his copper projects in Utah before construction on the mill began in 1912. The mill became operational in April, 1913, only fifteen months before World War I broke out in Europe. Production records are missing for most of 1913, but the first nine months ultimately proved to be a period of experimentation and adjustment.

Thankfully, good production records exist for five full years between January, 1914 and December, 1918. That was the mill's peak period of production and embraced the entire period of World War I. When examining those records, it becomes obvious that the Argo Mill had ramped up its production of lead and copper in later years. Those two metals ultimately amounted to almost 8% of its outgoing payments to mines.

During that time, the United States stockpiled enormous quantities of lead and copper for the war effort. Demand for both metals dropped and prices plummeted once the war ended in November, 1918.

Even before the end of the war, a recession had begun to grip the country. The collapse in base metal prices compounded economic problems for mine owners. Mines began closing one by one almost as soon as the Armistice was signed.

Unfortunately for Colorado's mining industry, mine closings were not limited to the area around the Argo Mill, but extended across the state. Sources of ore for the Argo Mill dried up within months and forced the mill to close in April, 1919, almost exactly on its sixth anniversary.[73]

The recession eased a bit in the latter part of 1919, but not enough for shuttered mines to notice. The situation was so bad that owners of the Argo sold both the mill and tunnel to Gem Mining Company in 1920. The United States soon fell into a deep depression that lasted until July, 1921.

There were several ownership changes after Gem's purchase. No mill records from that time are known to exist, so operations between December, 1918 and June, 1934 remain a mystery.

In January, 1934, global pressures forced the Federal government to devalue the U.S. dollar by 41%. It did that by raising the dollar's conversion rate into gold from $20.67 per troy ounce to $35.00. That huge jump in gold prices re-

No photos of the mill are currently known from the period immediately after it became operational. in 1913. It appears this image was might have been shot in an early 1930s winter after a light dusting of snow. No activity is evident—*Miller Collection, Historical Society of Idaho Springs.*

opened many gold operations around the state including some in Gilpin and Clear Creek counties.

A small batch of mill records survives to show an 18-month burst of activity between June, 1934 and December, 1935. Records after that period are lost, assuming the mill operated at all.

All told, six and a half years of mill records survive. It seems unlikely that sporadic production from missing years amounted to more than 5% of peak production. If true, the Argo Mill seems to have produced slightly over 60,000 troy ounces of gold and 500,000 ounces of silver during its lifespan.

	Precious metals produced by the Argo Mill (in troy ounces)			
	1914–1918	1934–1935	Other years	Total
Gold	53,318	4,150,	2,900*	60,368
Silver	427,477	48,609	24,000*	500,086
* estimated				

Did ore processing through the mill really dry up after 1935?

The truth is, we don't know for sure. Records are either missing because they were destroyed or because the mill was shuttered. The Colorado Bureau of Mines made no mention whatsoever of mill operations between 1935 and 1941. It reported the tunnel being operated by the Argo Mining Drainage Transportation & Tunnel Co. during 1941–1943, but again, there were no mentions of the mill or gold production, if any. It seems possible that the latter company may have milled some ore in conjunction with its workings in the Kansas vein while attempting to de-water the Kansas Mine overhead. Unless new information is found to the contrary, it currently *appears* mill operations stopped permanently at the end of 1935.

The Argo Mill was probably mostly intact at the time of the 1943 disaster. With the tunnel permanently closed, exposed wood was left to rot and the roof began rusting away. Vandals systematically removed windows with rocks and other projectiles until every pane was gone. This image shows new and unpainted sheets of galvanized roofing over several areas, suggesting this photograph dates from about 1977 after James Maxwell purchased the property and began restoration—*Historical Society of Idaho Springs.*

Build date	\multicolumn{2}{c}{November, 1912[75] to March, 1913}
Opening date	\multicolumn{2}{c}{about April 1, 1913}
Active period	\multicolumn{2}{c}{1913–1935}
Active periods	\multicolumn{2}{c}{January, 1914 to December, 1918 activity 1918 to 1935 unknown June, 1934 to 1935}
Plant capacity (per day) 1913–1915 1916–1921 after 1921	120 tons 200 tons unknown	109 tonnes 181 tonnes unknown
Ore storage capacity	1,600 tons	1,451 tonnes
Number stamps	\multicolumn{2}{c}{20}
Stamp weight (each)	1,050 pounds	476 killograms
Stamp drops	\multicolumn{2}{c}{100 per minute}
Drop distance	6 inches	15 centimeters
Gold recovery per period Apr., 1913 to Nov., 1913	approx. 60%	gravity, cyanidation, amalgamation
Dec., 1914 to Dec., 1915	approx. 90%	gravity, cyanidation, some amalgamation
Jan., 1916 to Jun., 1916	approx. 90%	gravity, flotation, cyanidation, some amalgamation
Jun., 1916 to Apr, 1919	approx. 92%	gravity, froth flotation, some amalgamation
after 1919	unknown	unknown
Ownership	Jul., 1912 to Nov., 1920 Nov., 1920	Argo Reduction and Ore Purchasing Co. Gem Mining Co.

SAMUEL NEWHOUSE

Samuel Newhouse was a 38-year old mining entrepreneur when he imagined the Argo Tunnel and set about to create it. Newhouse made himself into a millionaire through bold moves, but they weren't the moves of ordinary Western mining men; they seemed more like the moves of a chess player. He achieved success not by bluster and manipulation, but by friendship and constant work. "Constant" seems to be the operative word.

New York City and Scranton

Samuel's Jewish parents, Isaac and Battela Newhouse[81] had emigrated from Bavaria, probably around 1850. Samuel was born in New York City October 14, 1853,[82] the second of nine children. The Newhouse family moved to Scranton sometime before 1858,[83] a prosperous small city in the northern anthracite coal field of northeastern Pennsylvania where Isaac made his living as a tailor.[84]

The family of nine was complete when a census taker visited the Newhouses in July, 1870. Samuel was not quite seventeen, but was recorded as a law student.[85] That did not mean Newhouse was enrolled at a college, but rather was studying, or "reading," law under the tutelage of Scranton lawyers Aretus H. Winton and Edward N. Willard.[86]

Three and a half years later, lawyer Michael Zimmerman was appointed Clerk of the Courts of Luzerne County, Pennsylvania and chose Samuel Newhouse to be his chief clerk.[87] When Zimmerman's term ended in January, 1877, the *Scranton Republican* applauded his service and added that,

> "Mr. Samuel Newhouse, his efficient and courteous deputy, has also been justly accorded a full meed of praise for his careful execution of the duties devolving upon him and his polite and suave manner, observed alike among all with whom he associated. There are many who will regret their retirement from the Clerk's office; there are none who will not wish that their future may be most prosperous, and their associations with their fellows the most pleasurable."[88]

It is probably safe to assume that by the time he left public service Newhouse was familiar with property law, mining law, and miners.

Leadville and Ouray

Glowing newspaper reports about Leadville, Colorado caught the attention of Samuel and two Scranton friends, Sylvanus Ayres and Jacob Ridgeway Wright around 1878. Leadville, Colorado had been founded on lead mines, but was booming a second time with rich new silver discoveries. Hundreds of men were reaching Leadville every month, so the arrival of the three more men from Pennsylvania was never recorded, but was probably early in 1879.[89]

Sometime in 1880, the three formed a small local mining brokerage[90] named Ayers, Wright & Newhouse. Ayres' and Wright's connections with Scranton remained strong. Anthracite mining had built Scranton. Bankers there were comfortable with the mining industry, so investors from Scranton[91] financed the Merchants & Mechanics Bank in Leadville in the spring of 1879. By 1881, Ayres and Wright were on its board of directors,[92] but Newhouse's history is unclear. Several references say he tried his hand at lawyering, wallpaper sales, newspaper work, and mining.[93] Some stories are obviously exaggerated, but it is clear he had become secretary of a prominent mining company by 1881.

The office of Leadville Transfer Company was located behind the Merchants and Mechanics. Fred Rockwell had purchased the haulage company from founder Jim McGee around November, 1880. The company was a heavy advertiser in local newspapers and listed Rockwell as its manager. The partnership of Ayers, Wright & Newhouse disbanded in July of 1882[94] and advertisements promptly began listing Samuel Newhouse as the treasurer and manager of Leadville Transfer.[95]

It seems reasonable to assume that Newhouse's contacts with mining interests grew with his management of the transfer company. He must have done adequately well, because the company was renamed the Newhouse Transfer Company early in 1884.

Even rough and tumble towns like Leadville yearned for civility. Within months of Newhouse's arrival in Leadville, Horace Tabor opened his lavish Tabor Opera House. Shortly thereafter, the *Leadville Weekly Herald* began publishing its "Social Matters" column. It was not long before tidbits about young ladies began appearing, among them a Miss Ida Stingley.

Ida was born in Virginia, September 3, 1863, to parents Hiram Stingley and Mary A. Hotte.[96] Hiram passed away that same year, leaving Mary in the lurch with children Mollie, Richard, and baby Ida. For some unknown reason, Mary and her children moved west, first to Manhattan, Kansas,[97] then Boulder, Colorado[98] and finally Leadville. Ida made her first newspaper appearance January 12, 1881 in a tiny snippet in the *Leadville Daily Herald* that mentioned, "Miss Stingley and Miss Gruber were the best lady skaters at the Roller rink last night."[99]

The *Leadville Daily Herald's* social reporter found

Ida Stingley and Samuel Newhouse together at a party, December 16, 1882. Two weeks later, the same newspaper published a small notice at the bottom of page 1:

> "Denver, January 1—Mr. Samuel Newhouse and Miss Ida Stingley, both of your city, were married at the residence of the bride's sister, Mrs. George O. Moore, on Welton street, by the Rev. J. D. Hilton, at one o'clock to-day, and left on the 2:30 afternoon Chicago, Burlington and Quincy train for the east."[100]

For the next seven years, Samuel and Ida Newhouse left little evidence of their whereabouts and actions. There had been brief mentions in Leadville newspapers during 1881 of sales of "Ayres" and "Newhouse" claims in the Tellurium and Tillurick Districts (locations unknown) and the Tenmile District of Summit County, Colorado.[101] A few more spotty mentions of transfers of others Newhouse claims appeared throughout the 1880s. The Newhouse Transfer Company continued to run ads in Leadville newspapers until Samuel sold the business to Howie Brothers in September, 1886.[102] The generally accepted story in several biographies was that Samuel and Ida had moved to Ouray around 1883 where Newhouse became involved in gold mining.[103]

Newspapers in southwestern Colorado mentioned Newhouse only occasionally, usually reporting movements of "Sammy" and Mrs. Newhouse back and forth to the East. It seems likely that many of the trips were fundraising attempts. As a result, it appears Newhouse owned, probably in partnerships with others, several older mining properties around Silverton

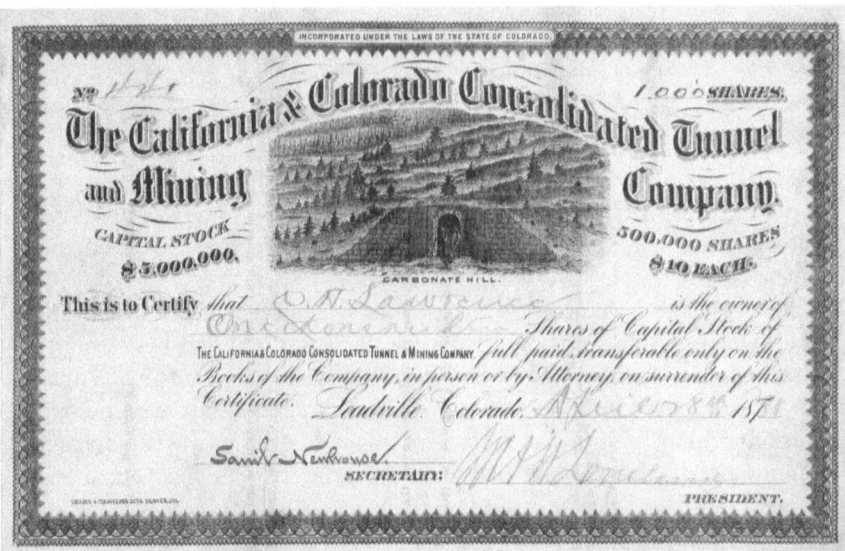

A rare stock certificate issued by the California & Colorado Consolidated Tunnel & Mining Company at Leadville, Colorado in April, 1881. Officers included William A. H. Loveland as president and Samuel Newhouse as secretary—*Holabird Western Americana Collections, LLC, Reno, Nevada, Big Tent Auction, Apr. 17, 2020, lot 2236.*

Newhouse was 27 years old when he signed the certificate shown on the previous page. The date of this photograph is unknown, but seems to represent a man of about that age—*Historical Society of Idaho Springs.*

and Ouray.[104] Confirmation of his holdings has proven elusive, but Newhouse was most commonly mentioned in connection with mines like Maid of the Mist, Wheel of Fortune[105] and Lost Lode (all in Ouray County.)[106] One reference even mentions J. Ridgeway Wright, his friend from Scranton, being a "New York representative" for the Wheel of Fortune Mine.[107]

There seems to be general agreement that Newhouse amassed a substantial wealth when he sold his mining properties in Ouray and San Juan Counties. It seems clear that while Newhouse had been involved with mining companies around Ouray, he had cultivated solid relationships with European investors within a very short span of time. Maybe it was all fortunate circumstance. Perhaps it was his "careful execution" and "polite and suave manner" that the *Scranton Republican* had seen a decade earlier. Maybe, as several short biographies suggest, it was his attractive young wife who nursed a wealthy British businessman back to health. Whatever the case, Newhouse's mining career, which had developed high in the mountains of southwestern Colorado, was ready to emerge into the media spotlight for the next thirty years.

Denver and Idaho Springs

After seemingly living as an apparition, Samuel Newhouse next appeared in print in 1889. The Denver city directory listed him as a broker living in Denver at the Albany Hotel with an office in the Essex Building.[108] One would surmise Newhouse was probably involved with mining properties. With the luxury of hindsight, it is also safe to assume he busied himself during 1889 and 1890 talking up Colorado opportunities with English investors.

Investment opportunities in Denver would certainly have included mining properties in Gilpin and Clear Creek counties. Gold and silver mines in those areas were not played out but were definitely suffering from lack of capital. A large smelter had been in place for twelve years on the north side of Denver, taking ore from mines along the Front Range. There was easy rail access to mining towns like Central City, Black Hawk, Idaho Springs, and Georgetown.

Newhouse would have seen no shortage of investment opportunities. Nor were there shortages of experienced labor. Transportation was in place. Capital was the only real challenge. Newhouse had amassed some money from his mines in the San Juan Mountains, but he had located a larger supply across the Atlantic Ocean.

British investors had long experience funding coal mines in England and railroads in Central America. Newhouse would have been well aware of coal mines northwest of Denver and railroad development all across Colorado. No route would have been enticing than one across the mountains from Denver to Salt Lake City.

Samuel Newhouse probably set his eyes upon all sorts of things, one of which was Denver itself. After living in Leadville and Ouray, it would have been clear that Denver was going to experience the most robust growth. Denver was a 30-year old bustling, growing city surrounded by plenty of land for expansion. With all that room for growth, the need for commuter transportation would have presented an obvious investment opportunity.

It was no accident then, that Newhouse associated himself with political powerhouse, William A. H. Loveland.

Newhouse had history with Loveland, because he had served as secretary for Loveland's California & Colorado Consolidated Tunnel & Mining Company while in Leadville.[109] Loveland had been in Colorado since the gold rush of 1859 and was well-known throughout the state. He had long experience in Colorado railroading, especially his Colorado Central Railroad. Having just platted the new city of Lakewood with his wife Miranda and partner Charles Welch, Loveland had decided a new rail line on the west side of Denver would be a great idea. Subsequently, Loveland, Welch, and a group of like-minded investors organized the Denver, Lakewood & Golden Railroad Company (DL&G) in July, 1890. Samuel Newhouse was among the original board of directors and was appointed the company's first vice-president.[110]

Although there is no apparent evidence of English financing of the DL&G in 1890, English principals formed the Denver Coal Company in November, 1of that year with Newhouse as its managing director.[111] The company bought the Tindale Mine[112] located six miles north of Golden, along the base of the foothills in the vicinity of today's Ralston Reservoir.

At about the same time, Newhouse acquired a lease on the Eureka gold mine just west of Central City. No information has been found to indicate whether English ownership was involved.

On February 5, 1891, Samuel Newhouse staked two claims on the north side of Clear Creek, a short distance east of Idaho Springs. He named one claim the "Argo Lode" and the other the "Argo Mill Site."[113] Newhouse never intended either claim to be mined for gold. Instead, Newhouse planned to use the claims as the portal location for a long tunnel he wanted to dig toward and under the Central City mining district.

Except for staking claims, he did nothing with the tunnel project during 1891. Most likely, Newhouse focused on managing a coal mine and getting the DL&G up and running. By the end of the year, the railroad company had purchased all of its rolling stock and laid most of its thirteen miles of track into Golden. It also managed to build up debt to the point where it needed more money.

In response, Newhouse went to London late in the year seeking additional funding. Part of his goal was to extend DL&G track a few miles further north to bring coal out of the Ralston Creek area. At some point, though, he and Loveland had concocted a more elaborate plan to use the DL&G as the seed for a greater railroad system that would ultimately cross the Rocky Mountains on its way toward Utah and Salt Lake City.

Newhouse returned to Colorado in the second week of January, 1892 with assurances of English capital backing. Colorado newspapers reported that he had secured promises to purchase $800,000 worth of DL&G bonds.[114] Their actual purchase amounted to $627,000.

The newspapers, of course, printed the news they were given. What they never knew was the closeness of the relationship between Newhouse and his English investors. In hindsight, it is abundantly clear that investors trusted Samuel Newhouse. Otherwise they would never have backed the D&LG and his subsequent projects over a period of several years.

Within a week of returning from London, Newhouse incorporated the Argo Mining, Drainage, Transportation and Tunnel Company (AMDT&T) in Colorado on January 27, 1893.[115] Company organizers were Newhouse, his younger brother Ancel, and Charles C. Parsons, a lawyer he had known since his Leadville days.

Three months later, on April 25,[116] the British investors created the Newhouse Tunnel Company, Limited in London. The purpose of that company was to acquire and hold stocks and bonds of the AMDT&T. In practice, the British company funded the American company by buying almost all of Argo stock shares and bonds.

In September, with funding in place, Newhouse located the position where the tunnel would begin. He received "patents" (full ownership versus claims) on his two claims October 12. He probably set miners to the task of hand-drilling the tunnel around the middle of November, 1893 and switched over

Samuel Newhouse (in center with bow tie) in an undated photograph of a tour group inside the Argo Tunnel—*Historical Society of Idaho Springs.*

to mechanical drilling at the beginning of 1894. Newhouse had officially named his project "Argo Tunnel," but the mining industry almost always reported the project as the "great Newhouse Tunnel." Work in the tunnel slowed and stopped at various times, but the further the tunnel progressed, the more its media coverage grew.

With the tunnel progressing northward, Newhouse switched back to railroad and coal mine matters. Samuel Newhouse soon became one of Colorado's millionaires of renown. Newspapers around the state loved to cover his acquisitions and comings and goings to London.

The media's biggest problem with Newhouse was that he was never larger than life. He was never an imposing physical or egotistical presence. He never made much noise. He never seemed to like the limelight. His strength was locating and extracting opportunities from existing properties. His success with Leadville Transfer unclear, but he seems to have done well with the Wheel of Fortune and other mines around Ouray, Colorado.

No doubt, he had the same thing in mind when he acquired the Prussian Mine and surrounding claims north of Boulder, Colorado in March, 1894.[117] He followed up with acquisitions of the Revenue Mine (Madison County,

One would think that a man like Samuel Newhouse would have been photographed many times. In fact, even snapshots of him are rare and he never seemed to be the focus of attention. There are even woodcut imitations of this frequently-reproduced formal portrait—*Used by permission, Utah State Historical Society.*

Montana) in April, 1895,[118] the Ute and Ulay Mines (Lake City, Colorado) in October, 1896,[119] and the Highland Boy Mine (southwest of Salt Lake City) the same month.

The Newhouse Tunnel made Samuel Newhouse a household name among the nation's mining community, but it was the Highland Boy, and another old Leadville relationship, that made him and his English backers rich.

Salt Lake City and Copper

Thomas Weir was yet another easterner drawn west by opportunity. He too reached Leadville in 1879. Unlike Newhouse, Weir quickly appeared in the Leadville newspapers in conjunction with mining claims. By October, 1884, Weir had worked his way up from surveyor[120] to accountant[121] to manager of the A.Y. Mine. A short while later he became manager of the adjacent Minnie Mine.[122]

Weir was apparently a good mine manager becasue the Granite Mountain copper mine at Butte, Montana managed to hire him away from Leadville in November, 1888.[123] No documentary evidence has appeared, but it seems probable that Newhouse and Weir had met and formed a mutual respect during their Leadville years. Weir spent the next five years managing the Granite Mountain Mine while Newhouse had involved himself with gold and silver mines in southwestern Colorado.

Weir resigned management of the Granite Mountain Mine around April, 1893 and moved to Salt Lake City early in 1894.[124] It is unclear how Newhouse and Weir re-connected or who initiated the reunion, but it is possible they had renewed their friendship while Newhouse was evaluating copper mines in Montana. Regardless, Weir became aware of the Highland Boy Mine in Bingham Canyon in 1895, probably while examining the workings of the adjacent Henry M. Mine in July.[125]

Highland Boy was a rather average gold mine located about twenty two miles (36 km) southwest of Salt Lake City and twelve miles (20 km) west of today's Riverton, Utah. Having extended experience in both gold and copper mines, Weir concluded that owners of the Highland Boy and adjacent claims had left significant amounts of gold in the ground. Weir and Newhouse decided to combine them all into one larger, more profitable mine.

Starting in mid-1895, Weir negotiated with owners of the Highland Boy Mine and surrounding claims and convinced them of the wisdom of selling. At some point, probably early in 1896, Newhouse went to London and arranged for his English friends to fund the promising gold project.

On October 3, 1896, with funding secured, Weir purchased the Highland Boy Mine, adjacent claims, water rights, and a mill site. He immediately conveyed all the parcels to Newhouse who wrote a $65,000 check for the down-payment and signed a promissory note to pay another $135,000 within six months.[126] $200,000 was a strong price for such a speculation and was one of Utah's most expensive mining transactions that year.

Newhouse organized the Highland Boy Gold Mining Company in New Jersey later that month[127] while Weir began mine planning. Meanwhile,

Newhouse's London investors formed Utah Consolidated Gold Mines, Limited (UCGM) under British law.[128] Similar to the earlier arrangement at the Argo Tunnel, UCGM's sole purpose was to fund the Highland Boy Gold Mining Company by purchasing its stocks and bonds.

Charles C. Parsons, one of the co-organizers of the Argo Tunnel, provided legal work on the deal. He left for Montana immediately after finalizing paperwork on Highland Boy to complete another Newhouse purchase near Butte. Once that agreement was in place, Parsons traveled to California to push forward yet another Newhouse deal for the Kennedy Mine near Jackson, California.[129]

The Highland Boy Mine had been a so-so gold mine. The surrounding claims had hardly been touched. It was not long after they got into the mine and started development in earnest that Weir and Newhouse realized there was an unusually high percentage of copper within their gold-silver ore zone. It did not take long before they decided that Highland Boy was actually more valuable as a copper mine than a gold mine.

Over the next few years, the Highland Boy deepened its shaft and began extracting three distinct copper-bearing veins from the property. The company carried ore down the canyon to a railroad via a two-mile long aerial tram. From there, trains transported ore to the Highland Boy Mill near Salt Lake City.

An undated but early photo of underground miners drilling and mucking in the Highland Boy copper mine—*David Johnson, www.miningartifacts.org.*

Facilities of the Highland Boy Mine in Bingham Canyon, Oquirrh Mountains, southwest of Salt Lake City—*Used by permission, Utah State Historical Society.*

The mine proved so profitable that it caught the eye of a big-time "player" in the copper business, a player with incredibly deep pockets. Identifying that company takes a bit of explaining.

Utah Consolidated Gold Mines. Ltd. (UCGM) owned the majority of Highland Boy Gold Mining Company stock. UCGM's board of directors included Samuel Newhouse, Urban H. Broughton and several Londoners. Broughton was the general manager of UCGM[130] and just happened to be married to the daughter of Henry Huttleston Rogers.

H. H. Rogers had amassed incredible wealth as one of the primary executives and stockholders of the giant Standard Oil Trust. That company had made John D. Rockefeller the richest man in America. The Standard Oil Trust owned another trust called Amalgamated Copper with an estimated worth in the range of $400,000,000. Amalgamated Copper owned many copper companies, among them the giant Anaconda Mining Company at Butte, Montana.[131]

Once made aware of Highland Boy's potential (through Rogers, of course) Amalgamated Copper shifted its focus to Highland Boy. It began quiet negotiations to acquire stock in the British holding company in 1898. By February, 1899,[132] newspapers and industry magazines began breaking the news that "Standard Oil interests" had acquired control of UCGM in one block of shares. The company never divulged exact details to the press, so

Newhouse at his prime, pulling the strings of Utah mining men and holding a fistful of new developments. Caricature from *Just for Fun: Cartoons and Caricatures of Men in Utah*, by E. A. Thompson. 1906. The man on Newhouse's left shoulder is holding a bag of British pounds and saying, "H'I say old man, won't you h'invest this for me?"—*Used by permission, Utah State Historical Society.*

there was much speculation and disagreement about the purchase price

It turned out that Amalgamated Copper had paid about $6,000,000 for half of the stock of UCGM. Newhouse subsequently resigned as president of Highland Boy and Weir resigned as general manager. It was rumored, although never publicly confirmed, that the majority of shares sold to Amalgamated had come from Newhouse and Weir. It took almost seven years for the Amalgamated to buy up remaining shares. Once under total control in May, 1907, managers re-organized UCGM (London) as Utah Consolidated Mining Co. in the state of New Jersey.

As soon as Amalgamated had begun eyeing Highland Boy for acquisition, Newhouse and Weir moved higher up Bingham Canyon and spent $300,000 acquiring a large group of claims adjacent to the Highland Boy group.[133] The new project was to be a "rinse and repeat" endeavor. Newhouse would organize a mining company under U.S. law and British investors would form a holding company in England. Copper reserves at the new project were larger but lower grade than Highland Boy. Making a profit mining low-grade ore was going to be more difficult.

With a new copper project under control, Newhouse sailed again for England in May, 1898 to chat with his investors. Together they formed Boston Consolidated Copper & Gold Mining Company, Limited.[134] Samuel Newhouse was installed as company chairman. Newhouse also signed on to be the company's managing director under a six-year contract. If successful in making the mine profitable, he would receive a percentage of profits.

Newhouse returned to Colorado a month later and promptly moved his operations to Salt Lake City.[135] Since Newhouse had been so active in Utah, his decision was a big story in that state's newspapers. Understandably, the Colorado press was reluctant to lose one of its prominent millionaires.

Newhouse and Weir organized the Boston Consolidated Mining Company in New York later in 1898 as the wholly-owned subsidiary of the British company.[136] Industry experts debated whether their copper reserves were too poor for profitable operation. Newhouse and Weir ignored naysayers and ultimately developed over two miles of underground workings by mid-1905. The following year, the mine began construction on a $1,500,000 mill to process and concentrate ore.

With a dedicated mill under construction, mine manager Lafayette Hanchett and superintendent Louis Cates considered how to take better advantage of the large reserves of low-grade ores they had under control. They continued working underground, but concluded they could save money by removing near-surface ore with steam shovels.

They put their first shovel to work in June, 1906.[137] It proved so successful that the company added four more shovels within a year. Engineers at the neighboring Utah Copper Company adopted the same mining method a few

November, 1906 view of a steam shovel at work at the Boston Consolidated Mine in Bingham Canyon—*Used by permission, Utah State Historical Society.*

months later. Together, the two companies perfected a strip mining method that persists to this day in the same location. That spot is now the great Bingham Canyon Mine, an open pit mine frequently called "The Richest Hole on Earth." The Bingham pit is currently three miles (5 km) wide, four miles (7 km) long and over three thousand feet (930 m) deep,

Shovel operations at Boston Consolidated ran into a different kind of ore sometime in 1907. The new ore was rich in iron and not fully compatible with the mill. No one had anticipated such a problem. In order to keep the mill working at maximum output, Hanchett and Cates had to produce more ore from the underground mine which raised costs. As if matters could not get worse, a panic hit the New York stock market in May, 1907. As the market dropped, the cost of borrowing operating funds rose.

Even as early as 1905, management in both Boston Consolidated and its rival Utah Copper had realized they would need to merge at some point if either company hoped to survive. Utah Copper (not to be confused with Amalgamated's Utah Consolidated) was backed by wealthy Guggenheim interests and had the financial resources to wait out Boston Consolidated's English investors. Although the companies controlled similar amounts and qualities of copper reserves, Boston was financially weaker. Newhouse and Weir finally relented in 1909 and convinced their English backers to sell out to Utah Copper on January 26, 1910.

Other projects

No one could ever accuse Newhouse of being single-minded. He had been involved with Bingham Canyon copper since 1896, but had not abandoned his other investments. Far from it.

Newhouse had remained a director of the Denver, Lakewood & Golden Railroad back in Colorado. Perhaps because of his intense involvement with copper, Newhouse had never succeeded in convincing a sufficient number of investors that the DL&G was going to be the best company to push a new rail route over the mountains.

Newhouse and Weir had acquired an iron mine at Tintic, Utah in April, 1899.[138] The next month, Newhouse and one of his brothers acquired an interesting piece of land in New York City. In June, 1899, Newhouse and Weir bought claims in Utah's famous Mercur gold district.[139]

Newhouse interests outside of Utah included mines in Montana, California, New Mexico, and Idaho. The Argo Tunnel had never required much oversight. Not wanting to be left out, Colorado newspapers circulated rumors of another Newhouse tunnel project at Red Cliff northwest of Leadville.[140] Industry gossip sheets loved reporting about Newhouse, but he probably owned stock in more companies and had more projects underway than any of them ever knew about.

Aside from his heavy involvement at Bingham Canyon at the time, Newhouse's winded activity in 1900 had been pretty much a repeat of 1899. Reports of Newhouse involvement in digging a 3,000-foot tunnel at Red Cliff re-emerged in May.[141] That month, the Salt Lake Telegram published more rumors of his intent to extend the DL&G through Boulder and Steamboat Springs to Salt Lake. Although little was mentioned of it later, Newhouse headed a syndicate that procured coal, timber, and precious metals rights on three huge concessions in China during its Open-Door policy.[142]

When examining his projects one at a time, Newhouse comes across as calm and insightful. If there were examples of cavalier or impulsive behavior, they never made it into newspapers or biographies. At least not at that time.

Considering all his various projects together, Newhouse seems like a whirlwind in a well-tailored suit. It makes one tired to read about his incessant activities and acquisitions. One can only wonder how he handled the boredom of being trapped on ships for a week or more while sailing back and forth to London.

Over the years, a mythology has grown around one of Newhouse's off-topic investments. Although tiny in comparison with most of his mining deals, it proved highly important in foreshadowing his later career.

Manhattan real estate deal

Samuel's brother Mott owned several pieces of property in New York City and was no doubt familiar with a small, triangular piece of land called Eno's Corner located at the intersection of Broadway, Fifth Avenue, and 23rd

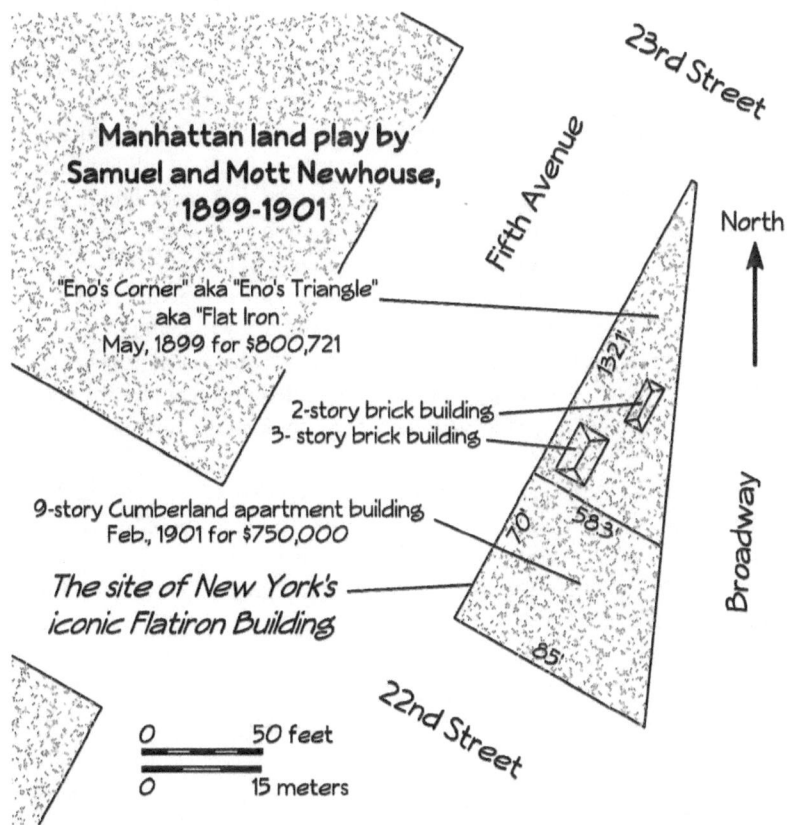

Street. The Manhattan tract held two old brick buildings, one two stories tall and the other three floors. Together the structures generated about $42,000 in rent each year. Amos Eno's son William had purchased the property from his father's estate for $690,000 in April, 1899,[143] a price higher than its rental income would have justified.

Samuel Newhouse was in and out of New York frequently, but it seems unlikely the Eno purchase would have caught his attention had it not been for his brother. After all, Highland Boy had sold only a couple months before and he was in the middle of creating Boston Consolidated. Nonetheless, Samuel and Mott bought the triangle for $800,721,[144] thereby giving William Eno a profit of almost $111,000 in one month. To outside observers, the purchase smacked of unbridled speculation.

The editor opined in the May 6, 1899 issue of the *Real Estate Record and Builders'* weekly magazine that,

> "...the triangle was bought by a millionaire mine owner from the West, who parted with his money simply because of the attractiveness of the parcel as an investment for large capital, and his action suggests the idea that the economic influences which made this particular holding seem desirable for the purpose of investment are becoming manifest to men of means as regards Manhattan business property generally."[145]

The editor had a point. Aggressive development seemed unlikely for a piece of property that totaled less than 3,900 square feet. A *square* parcel of land that size today would be adequate for a small, 14-car parking lot.

If significant development were to be attempted, someone would need to combine the triangle with another odd-shaped piece of land adjoining on the south side. That property was home to a nine-story apartment building called the Cumberland.[146] Newhouse ultimately purchased the Cumberland property for a reported $750,000, but not until the middle of February, 1901.

With the whole block under control, development seemed a bit more reasonable. But only a bit. The shape of the property was *not at all* ideal. The combined property was a narrow *triangle*, with its apex at the intersection of Broadway and Fifth Avenue. Although it extended 200 feet (61 m) south, it was only 85 feet (26 m) wide at its base. What could someone do with a parcel shaped like that?

Rumors circulated that Newhouse wanted to erect a 20–25-story building[147] on that small sliver of land. Most observers thought the idea ridiculous, certain that the wind would topple such a spindly building.

Anyone who knew Newhouse would have recognized that something was indeed "in the wind." This time, it was a deal with the George A. Fuller Company, a high-rise builder from Chicago. The Fuller Company had quietly formed a New York subsidiary called Cumberland Realty Company. Its purpose was to erect a building on the triangle owned by Newhouse.

Around the first of March, 1901, two weeks after purchasing the Cumberland apartment and land, Newhouse sold his two parcels to Cumberland Realty for $1,740,000.[148] On paper, Newhouse pocketed about

Looking south-southwest toward the pointed end of the Flatiron Building in 1910, when it was still known as the Fuller Building—*Irving Underhill, Public domain, via Wikimedia Commons.*

$189,000 in profit minus expenses. Newhouse was also a member of the original board of directors of Cumberland Realty Company,[149] so it seems likely that he made additional unrecorded profit elsewhere in the deal.

To everyone's surprise, construction on the Fuller Building began almost before ink had dried on closing papers. Obviously, the Fuller Company had already completed much of the building design. The skeleton of the 21-story triangular building went up at the rate of about a floor a week and the building was finished in June, 1902[150] and ready for occupancy in October.

Because of its shape, many New Yorkers had known Eno's Triangle as "The Flat Iron" for years. Although officially named the Fuller Building, people were calling it "The Flatiron Building" even before completion. The name stuck and the building remains one of New York's most iconic and photographed architectural landmarks.

It seems unlikely that Newhouse ever lost a minute's sleep over this real estate deal. It would never have required a lot of attention and it made him a decent profit. If only his future real estate ventures were to turn out so well. It seems his experience with the Fuller Company had made development look too easy.

Next?...

Seemingly addicted to copper, Newhouse rolled the dice once more. This time, he tried his luck rehabilitating a copper property in the San Francisco Mountains of Beaver County, Utah. In this case, he paid $200,000 in October, 1901 for the old Cactus Mine and surrounding claims. To develop the property, he organized the Newhouse Mines & Smelters Company in New York in May, 1903.[151] No evidence of English investment in this project has emerged.

The mill of the Cactus Mine at Newhouse, Utah in August, 1908. It seems to be a quiet day with the company's locomotive sitting idle beside the smelter. One might wonder that if the project were supposed to be so capable of making money, where was the smoke?—*Used by permission, Utah State Historical Society.*

During this period, practically everything Newhouse did made news—and money. Even his purchase of an old copper project in the desert of southwestern Utah attracted the attention of a newspaper in a small town in upstate New York. The *Richfield Springs Mercury* (Oct. 27, 1904) carried an article about Newhouse, saying he had announced the discovery of an $85 million deposit at the Cactus Mine. It went on to say that he intended to initiate a profit sharing plan with his miners and that each would receive a 200 ft x 600 ft (61 x 183 m) lot and house.

Over the next several years, Newhouse built an elaborate mill, a 3-mile railroad and the entire town of Newhouse to support the operation. Operations never turned out as profitably as planned and the Panic of 1907 probably hurt Newhouse's ability to raise necessary operating funds. With his name prominently attached to the company, the town, and the railroad, every penny drop in stock price ended up as a black mark against Newhouse. After all, Newhouse and his stockholders had dumped several millions of dollars into a second-rate project in the desert. One wonders whether he might have spent sleepless nights pondering the Cactus project.

Regardless of Newhouse's promises that the mine was on the verge of profitability, stock prices of Newhouse Mines fell with disappointing regularity. It was like watching a car crash in slow motion. The company had no ability to repay debt, so creditors foreclosed the company in December, 1909 and reorganized it as South Utah Mines and Smelters.[152]

All the while Newhouse had been planning his strategy to buy and revive the Cactus Mine, principals and creditors in the Denver, Lakewood & Golden Railroad[153] finally realized the company was never going to be a success. It had never attracted sufficient freight or passenger traffic between its namesake cities. It had scraped by, but had never paid interest to its English bondholders. When it became clear the property would finally be foreclosed and sold, Newhouse formed a syndicate to buy out the original bonds and take over the assets. It incorporated a new company in 1904 named Denver & Intermountain Railway. Newhouse became its first president.[154]

Considering everything that was going on in Newhouse's empire, one could question whether it had been wise to take on another presidency, especially the presidency of a railroad.

The days of rapacious railroading were fading fast. Jay Gould was dead. Commodore Vanderbilt and his son William Henry were dead. Railroading had matured to the point where cutthroat penny-pinchers were sitting in the re-upholstered chairs of the cutthroat robber barons.

Samuel Newhouse had the personality of neither. He was a mining man, pure and simple.

It was a good thing he owned a private rail car. As a mining man, Newhouse seemed to be needed everywhere. Here is a mere sampling of his known responsibilities during his busiest period between 1904 and 1907 (his role at the Argo project, if any during that time, is unknown):

Newhouse's private railcar from a glass plate negative produced by Shipler Commercial Photographers, December 1, 1905—*Used by permission, Utah State Historical Society.*

The photo below shows a gathering of the University Club at the Roof Top Garden atop the Hotel Utah, May 5, 1904. Samuel Newhouse is seated at left—*Used by permission, Utah State Historical Society.*

- Bingham Central Mining Co. (Utah, president)
- Bingham Central Standard Copper Co. (Utah, president)
- Bingham Mines Co. (Utah, director)
- Boston Consolidated Copper & Gold Mining Co., Ltd. (Utah, managing director)
- Boston Consolidated Mining Co. (Utah, managing director)
- Butte Copper Exploration Co. (Montana, role unknown)
- Denver & Intermountain Railway Co. (Colorado, director and president)
- Dominion Copper Co. (British Columbia, general manager)
- Grand Gulch Copper Mining Co. (Arizona, general manager)
- Louisiana Consolidated Gold Mining Co. (president)
- Lucky Boy Mine (Montana, manager)
- Majestic Copper Co. (Utah, general manager)
- Montana Boy Consolidated Mines Co. (president)
- Montana Revenue Gold Mining Co. (part owner)
- Montgomery Mountain Mining Co. (president)
- Newhouse Mines & Smelters Co. (Utah, president)
- Nipissing Mining Co. (Ontario, director and president)
- Ohio Kentucky Mining Co. (Nevada, president)
- Silver King Consolidated Mining Co. (Idaho, vice president)
- Western Nevada Copper Co. (Nevada, founder)

Newhouse's strengths were in mining. He was a deal maker. He knew metals and he knew the metals market. He understood its cycles. He recognized competent people and he knew which ones to partner with. He made friends easily and he kept them. He knew how to talk to investors and soothe their worries. People liked him and they trusted him.

In 1906, however, the restless Samuel Newhouse decided to change his stripes—or at least add new ones. He decided to become a real estate developer. It seems he had caught the real estate bug through his earlier involvement with the Flatiron Building.

Newhouse the Real Estate Developer

On the surface, real estate development seemed a natural extension of his vast experience. Miners and real estate developers both require land. Newhouse could never have mined a spoonful of dirt had he not controlled land. He knew how to do that very well. But was that knowledge sufficient? Was renting a square foot of office space the same thing as selling a pound of copper? Real estate seems a much less risky business than mining, but was there a point at which adding another element of risk reached a tipping point?

Newhouse turned his efforts to building and developing Salt Lake City, seemingly at the expense of mining. Most of all, he wanted to remake Exchange Place into a Salt Lake City version of Wall Street with gleaming office buildings and a grand hotel.

In November, 1906, Newhouse hired Chicago architect Henry Ives Cobb to plan and design eleven buildings. The first plans off Cobb's drawing board were two mirror-image Beaux Arts buildings four blocks south of Temple Square. At

An Edward Mitchell postcard view looking east at the Boston (left) and Newhouse (right) Buildings on South Main Street in Salt Lake City, Utah. The street in the center is Exchange Place and is now a pedestrian mall. Note the differences in the street-level facades—*Author's collection.*

eleven-stories each, the Boston Building and the Newhouse Building were to be the first skyscrapers to rise above Salt Lake City.[155]

Construction began on the Boston Building in 1907, followed by the Newhouse Building in 1908. Like the Flatiron Building back in Manhattan, each took about a year to complete. Both structures were still under construction in the spring of 1908 when it became apparent that Newhouse's plans had grown more grandiose.

> "In all, there are fifteen buildings which Mr. Newhouse plans to erect on his property in the new business district as rapidly as the growth of the city warrants."[156]

The next project to break ground was the Newhouse Hotel. It was to be another impressive eleven-story structure adorned with bronze and marble. It was going to have a two-story lobby, restaurant, café, luxurious amenities, and would open in 1911. The *Deseret Evening News* reported that Newhouse had planned to be present for ground-breaking on the morning of April 19, 1909, but had been "called to New York" the night before.

Admittedly, Newhouse had the hallmarks of someone who disliked cameras. But still, what had been so important as to take him away from breaking ground on his crown jewel project? The hotel was to be the opulent center stage for his next opus in life. Couldn't he have just said, "No?"

It was true that spaces in the Newhouse and Boston buildings had not been renting as well as expected. The Panic of 1907 had no doubt adversely affected Salt Lake City business. Was the impending bankruptcy of the Cactus project on his mind, especially since Newhouse, Utah bore his name? Was there a problem with one of his other numerous commitments? Samuel

Newhouse would never have considered the possibility at the time, but whatever problem pulled him away from Salt Lake that Sunday night may have portended problems yet to come.

While exact identifications are difficult to confirm, Newhouse is generally credited with constructing thirty buildings in Salt Lake City over the next few years. Additionally, he set about on a residential project and beautification effort on the south side of Salt Lake City and a development in Federal Heights on the northeast side.

Was his frenetic pace of development, generally funded by his own wallet, simply too fast? Was he letting his mining properties slip?

Perhaps as a way of questioning the wisdom of his real estate ventures without actually saying so, the *Denver Post* ran a story in October, 1910 saying that Samuel Newhouse was ready to move back to Colorado. The *Post* contended that he was fed up with the lack of support from Salt Lake political and business interests. The rumor proved false, but it was still true that Salt Lake's growth had been disappointingly slow by comparison to Utah's other cities north of Salt Lake City.

The Newhouse Hotel's predicted two-year completion proved overly optimistic. Contractors were ready and willing to work, but Newhouse's bank account was not. Even after six years, the hotel was still unfinished in the summer of 1914. Windows in the upper stories lacked glass and jokes circulated openly that the Newhouse Hotel was the "best air-conditioned hotel in the West."

Newhouse had never given up on developing natural resources, but his mining empire seems to have taken a turn when he shifted into real estate development. Newhouse Mines & Smelters had failed, but he continued trying to revive the Cactus Mine under the new South Utah Mines & Smelters Corp. He continued to throw money at copper projects like Walker Mining Company and others.

While perhaps seeming a bit harsh, it is fair to ask whether it was wise to invest in copper, *anywhere*, especially after helping create the largest copper mine in the world. Considering the amount of copper coming out of Bingham Canyon and Anaconda pit at Butte, one could question whether there was room in the world economy—and in the price of copper—for another copper mine. Let alone a copper mine that had already gone bankrupt once.

Industry reports about Newhouse's mining ventures were as quiet in the years after the hotel's ground-breaking as they had been celebratory in the years before. It was like a multi-year Sunday morning after a multi-year Saturday night. It was clear that Samuel Newhouse's media star was fading,

But his wife's was not.

In many ways, Ida Stingley Newhouse is a mystery. At least on this side of the Atlantic.

Delightful and fanciful stories about her abound. She was supposed to have been an entertaining and beguiling fixture at the court of King Edward VII. If reports in America were to be believed, she was more of a friend to King Edward than a mere event guest. Even New York newspapers mentioned her

Looking southwest toward the Newhouse Hotel at the corner of University Boulevard and South Main Street in Salt Lake City, October 26, 1915. The Boston and Newhouse Buildings are just a half block to the right of where the photographer stood—*Used by permission, Utah State Historical Society.*

attendance at the coronation of King George V in 1911. At the end of each London "season," she would return to Salt Lake with incredible clothes and even more incredible tales.

> "After a few days spent here, Mr. Newhouse will return to the east but Mrs. Newhouse will remain some time visiting her mother and other relatives in this city. It has been several years since Salt Lake was favored with a visit from Mrs. Newhouse, one of the most charming and interesting women who ever graced Salt Lake Society. In London she is one of the few untitled women who has gained and held a favored place in the ultra-smart set of the English metropolis. Her many friends are hoping that her visit will be a prolonged one."[157]

Ida liked New York City. She certainly enjoyed her custom-made Parisian outfits more. By all accounts, she loved displaying her gowns and pearls in London's high society most of all. After years of hobnobbing with Earls, Ladies, Lords, and monarchs, one can imagine that a copper king might have struggled to hold her attention. Even one attempting to re-make a city.

Still, the hammer was dropping on the Newhouse fortune. Slowly. Quietly. Without fanfare and without clear evidence of causation.

Winding down

By 1914, it was clear that Newhouse's wealth was eroding. Several writers have said that Newhouse went bankrupt, but none offered proof. Where is the evidence? Where is the bankruptcy filing? Where are the court declarations? And *where* are reports in newspapers? Reporters were always ready to pile on at the whiff of a great man being laid low. In short, where are the hundreds of articles the insatiable media would have written about Newhouse's demise?

There seems to be some agreement that Newhouse's fortune probably peaked at about $25,000,000,[158] roughly equivalent in spending power to $300 million or more today.

It also seems true that the huge Butte and Bingham Canyon copper mines were driving small mines and old districts toward extinction. Still, copper prices were rising with every bullet fired in Europe's new war. A rising tide would have raised all boats and Newhouse's boat was made out of copper. Adjusting for inflation, copper prices were higher in the World War I years of 1917 and 1918 than anytime before or since. Theoretically, Newhouse should have owned loads of shares in copper mines and reaped their dividends.

So where was Newhouse's wealth going?

It seems likely Newhouse's customary lending sources in London evaporated. On balance, it seems that Newhouse made substantial money in copper for most of his investors. However, Denver Coal Company had failed in the 1890s and they had never made money on the Denver Lakewood & Golden Railroad. It is likely they lost money when they sold out their positions in the Argo Tunnel in 1908. To top it all off, Newhouse's investors had been among the moneyed aristocracy. The World War had probably penalized them more than they realized at the time.

There had been five short-run recessions in the United States between 1902 and 1921. Anyone with significant money in the market had been affected.

Then, of course, there was Samuel's obsession with real estate development. A hundred thousand dollars in unpaid rents here, a half million spent in construction there, and pretty soon he would have felt serious drains on his wealth.

When considering Newhouse's finances, someone is bound to consider Ida's European adventures. She traveled constantly. She required huge and expensive Parisian wardrobes each social season. She was at home in their Salt Lake mansion only a few months a year and frequently less than that. The cost of her trans-Atlantic travel hobby could not have been trivial. However, there is absolutely no printed evidence to suggest that Newhouse was ever displeased with her.

What assets did Newhouse own that were making money in the 1920s? The media had reported no winning projects for Newhouse since the sale of Boston Consolidated in 1910. While never a topic to discuss in polite society, Newhouse might have been a multi-millionaire, but he had never amassed the vast wealth of John D. Rockefeller or Commodore Vanderbilt. Consequently, he did not have as far to fall.

MRS. NEWHOUSE
Of New York, who is staying at Claridge's Hotel for the season.

Ida Hotte Stingley Newhouse was a most elusive photographic subject, equally as elusive as her husband. This image comes from *The King*, an illustrated magazine published in London, June 21, 1902.

Virtually all biographies of Samuel and Ida state they separated in 1914 and there is no reason to suggest otherwise.

Yet, if there had been an impending separation in the marriage, it seemed oddly amicable.

> "Mrs. Samuel Newhouse who will leave for New York today (Feb. 14, 1914) gave an informal tea for her friends on Wednesday, sort of a farewell affair to those who have welcomed her in various ways and regret her departure. She will sail again within a few weeks where she will remain during the season and later go to Paris to be with the mother and sisters of Mr. Newhouse there."[159]

By the middle of June, 1914, Newhouse had successfully borrowed money to complete the Newhouse Hotel. He re-started construction and drove it through to completion. Unlike his disappearance from the hotel's groundbreaking ceremony, Newhouse was on site all day to welcome guests and gawkers to its grand opening on March 27, 1915.[160] Later that year, Newhouse sold the family mansion and moved into the Newhouse Hotel.

Because of the war, rumors had swirled that Mrs. Newhouse would return to Salt Lake during the summer, but she did not sail from Europe until October,

1915. With the mansion gone, she too moved into a suite at the Newhouse Hotel that Samuel had specially prepared for her.

Ida stayed in Salt Lake City until February, 1916 and purposely attended more social events than usual. She commented that the attitude in England had been depressing after the war began, made even worse because of the loss of so many friends. Prior to her leaving England the previous October, King George V had appointed her governess of military hospitals. She took the appointment seriously and every bit of disturbing news about the war made her more anxious to get back to England to start work.

Samuel, was greatly about her safety crossing the Atlantic again. Ida had seen German submarines on her October trip and German threats had only grown more serious. In February and March, 1916, Newhouse sent several telegraphs to her in New York, begging her to reconsider going to England. Newhouse released her last reply to the Salt Lake City press:

> "I must go to England and care for the boys who are suffering. I cannot add probably to their aid in any large degree, but I will be carrying out the work assigned me. England's aristocracy is shattered by this war and it is the people who rule. It is to them I go and also to the people of France, who have braved the hosts of the enemy empire. I do not care for the slackers who have shown the 'white feather,' nor for those like William Waldorf Astor who bought his title; I care not for the German mines or their submarines, but if you wish it I will wait until I see the developments from now until March 11. I have determined that I can do better work there (in the hospitals) than I can here."[161]

Ida made it to England safely by the end of March, 1916, but did not return to Salt Lake until December, 1918,[162] after the Armistice had been signed.

Industry journals had reported in January, 1917 that Newhouse had taken control of Magma Superior Copper Company in Arizona followed by rumors of a negotiation to purchase the Butte-Bullwhacker copper mine near Butte.

The next month, Newhouse sold both the Boston and Newhouse Buildings for $850,000 apiece.[163] There were whispers, but no conclusive proof, that Samuel Newhouse needed the money.

In September of 1917, at age 64, he appeared in oil industry magazines as president of the Casper-Embar Petroleum Company. The company reportedly controlled 4,000 acres of oil-bearing land in the Powder River Basin of northeastern Wyoming.[164] Only a few months later, early in 1918, he pulled out of the company after learning that management had been reckless in using stockholders' money for exploration.

With peace restored, Newhouse sailed to Europe late in the spring of 1919, and visited his sister Hattie Newhouse at Marnes la Coquette, a western suburb of Paris. Samuel's brother Mott had purchased Château de Marnes for their mother about twenty years before. It had been the chateau of Louis the XVI,[165] His sister had taken over the residence after their mother's death there in 1916.

Newhouse returned to Utah in June and stayed at the Newhouse Hotel until at least October, 1919. During that time, Newhouse sold his interest in the hotel to the Bonneville Hotel Company which had been operating the property under lease.[166] His whereabouts and actions after that time are sparsely documented.

Passport records show Newhouse traveled to Paris in January, 1921 and returned to Salt Lake in July, 1923. The *Salt Lake Mining Review* was ecstatic to report that Newhouse had not abandoned mining during his absence. It said that Newhouse was on his way to Mexico to examine the El Socorro Mine and had stopped in Utah to visit friends.[167] Newhouse was interested in buying the mine and was having engineers test its gold and silver possibilities.[168] Was he was thinking about re-working an old mine in Mexico in the same way he had amassed his formative wealth in Ouray?

After visiting the mine, he swung around to southern California and visited Ida in Beverly Hills. By this time, Samuel was seventy years old and Ida was sixty. No one could have argued they had not lived interesting and rich lives since meeting in Leadville forty years before.

Newhouse passed through Salt Lake again on his way back to New York and France. Friends must have wondered whether Samuel had contracted a case of "gold fever." They were probably convinced of that supposition after learning he had accepted the presidency of the Idaho Gold Corporation in November, 1923.[169] Would there be a new chapter in the Newhouse saga?

The saga was not to be. Newhouse resigned from Idaho Gold barely two months later.[170]

Seemingly still adhering to a brisk travel schedule, he returned to Salt Lake in April, 1924. During his visit, he fell ill and was admitted to the St. Mark's Hospital for a short stay. Upon recuperation in the Newhouse Hotel,[171] Samuel Newhouse left Salt Lake City for the last time. The next month, Newhouse dropped his option on El Socorro.[172] In describing Newhouse's travel plans back to France, the *Salt Lake Mining Review* suggested he would probably not attempt another mining venture because of failing health.[173]

Passport records suggest Newhouse came back to the United States again in November, 1924,[174] but records are lacking to explain the trip's purpose or when he returned to Europe. He was subsequently issued a new U. S. passport in 1926,[175] and crossed the Atlantic again. No records have been found to suggest he ever left France after that voyage..

Ida Newhouse was dramatically more cosmopolitan than Samuel, so her travel schedule always provided fodder for Salt Lake City social columns. Snippets show she made frequent trips between Los Angeles, Salt Lake and New York City during the 1920s.

She made at least one trip to England and France in May and June of 1925.[176] It is enticing and maybe a bit romantic to assume the French portion of her trip included Paris and an eight-mile cab ride to visit Samuel at Château de Marnes. If true, it was probably the last time Samuel and Ida were together after forty-two years of marriage.

Samuel Newhouse died of heart failure at a Paris clinic near his sister's château on Monday evening, September 22, 1930 at age 76. His sister, Hattie Newhouse, arranged his burial in the Newhouse family plot at Saint Germain-en-Laye.[177]

Ida died of pneumonia as a result of a virus at the West Haven Sanitarium in Los Angeles, California on Thursday, March 17, 1955.[178] She was 91 and had outlived her husband by twenty-five years.

The American Consulate in Paris filed this report of Samuel Newhouse's death, essentially a stand-in for an American death certificate. The report recorded his burial at a communal cemetery at Saint Germain-en-Laye. It seems curious that the Consulate-General did not notify Samuel's widow.

TIMELINE OF MINING AND RELATED EVENTS

1858—William Russell and band of 104 prospectors find gold along Cherry Creek, Ralston Creek and South Platte River; reports of their discoveries set off the first Colorado gold rush.

1859, Jan. 7—George Jackson discovers first placer gold in the mountains at today's Idaho Springs.

1859, May 6—John H. Gregory and party of Indiana prospectors claim the first gold-bearing vein deposit and set off a second gold rush.

1859, July—Several thousand people in Central City area during summer; 1,500 winter over in the area.

1861—Gilpin County (the smallest), Clear Creek County (second smallest) and Colorado Territory organized; Civil War begins; some gold mines close because of difficulty recovering gold.

1862—Investors and speculators organize numerous companies in the East to mine in Colorado; last mention of John Gregory around Central City; miners widely recognize problems with sulfides.

1863—Numerous Gilpin County mines close because of inability to retrieve gold from sulfide-rich ores; many placer operations in Gilpin exhausted, but continue in Clear Creek; lode deposits discovered near Idaho Springs and Empire.

1868—Boston & Colorado smelter begins operation at Black Hawk; mining begins to recover throughout the district; dynamite introduced.

1870—Colorado & Southern standard gauge railroad reaches Golden.

1872—Colorado Central narrow gauge railroad reaches Black Hawk (Dec. 11).

1873—Panic and "Long Depression" (Oct., 1873–Mar., 1879); gold production slackens; rail building stops; Denver Smelting Company builds plant at Denver; Boston & Colorado smelter at Black Hawk adds refining.

1876—Colorado becomes thirty-eighth state.

1877—Colorado Central reaches Idaho Springs (Jun. 12) and Georgetown (Aug. 14).

1878—Boston & Colorado Smelting Company builds new plant near Denver and closes Black Hawk plant; Colorado Central railroad reaches Central City (May 20).

1879—Mechanical mining drill introduced.

1893—Gilpin Tramway reaches most major mines in region; Silver Crash and Wall Street Panic; operations begin on Argo ("Newhouse") Tunnel at Idaho Springs.

1895—Accidental connection with flooded mine kills fourteen miners in the Americus and Sleepy Hollow mines near Black Hawk.

1897—Water successfully added to air drills to control dust.

1899—American Smelting and Refining Company (ASARCO) organized; Colorado & Southern Railroad acquires Colorado Central.

1906—Colorado Southern Railroad purchases the Gilpin Tramway and renames it Gilpin Railroad.

1908—Decreased gold production from Gilpin County begins.

1909—Fire destroys part of the Boston & Colorado ("Argo") smelter.

1910—Argo Tunnel completed, 4.16 miles long; Boston & Colorado ("Argo") smelter closes permanently.

1913—Argo Mill opens at the mouth of the Argo Tunnel.

1917—Gilpin Railroad discontinues service.

1918—Post-WWI recession (Aug., 1918–Mar., 1919)

1920—Depression of 1920 (Jan., 1920–Jul., 1921)

1925—Colorado & Southern discontinues service to Central City.

1929—Wall Street stock market crash (Oct. 24 and 29.)

1932—Depth of Great Depression (1929–1941 per Federal Reserve.)

1934—Government raises price of gold to $35 per ounce; dredge operations start on Clear Creek.

1941—Colorado & Southern discontinues rail service west of Golden and removes tracks.

1943—Miners accidentally blast into water-filled Kansas Mine; resulting flood kills four; Argo Tunnel never reopens.

1968—United States drops gold standard; price of gold allowed to "float" with world demand; new interest in gold mining proves short-lived.

1976—James Maxwell buys Argo Tunnel and Mill and begins restoration.

1980—Huge discharge from tunnel sends acidic water down Clear Creek.

1998—EPA plant to treat water from Argo Tunnel operational.

2012—EPA water treatment plant further upgraded.

2015—EPA installs bulkhead in Argo Tunnel to prevent future floods.

REFERENCES

anonymous, undated, *Underground Workings Near North End of Argo Tunnel, Clear Creek, County, Colorado*, Colorado School of Mines, Mine Maps – Mines Library Special Collections, Archives.

anonymous, undated, *Newhouse Tunnel Vicinity Mining Claims and Underground Workings,* (Gem and Freighter's Friend mines), Clear Creek County, Colorado, Colorado School of Mines, Mine Maps – Mines Library Special Collections, Archives.

Alexiou, Alice Sparberg, 2010, *The Flatiron: The New York landmark and the incomparable city that arose with it.*

Argo Reduction and Ore Purchasing Company, 1914-1918 and 1934-1935, *Record of Ore Purchased,* ledgers showing amounts or ore purchased and correlated analyses

Ballenger and Richards, 1889, *Ballenger & Richards 17th Annual Denver City Directory.*

Bastin, Edson S. and James M. Hill, 1917, *Economic Geology of Gilpin County and Adjacent Parts of Clear Creek and Boulder Counties, Colorado*, United States Geological Survey Professional Paper 94.

Boulder Daily Camera, various issues and dates, newspaper published at Boulder, Colorado.

Bradley, Martha Sonntag, 1999, *A History of Beaver County.*

Carbonate Chronicle, The, various issues, newspaper published at Leadville, Colorado.

Chaffee, Maurice A., 1972, *Distribution and Abundance of Gold and Other Selected Elements in Altered Bedrock, Empire Mining District, Clear Creek, Colorado,* United States Geological Survey Bulletin 1278-C.

Collins, George E., 1882-1946, *Collins Papers,* collection housed at Western History/ Genealogy Department, Denver Public Library.

Colorado Bureau of Mines, various dates, *Annual Report.*

Colorado Bureau of Mines, various dates, *Inspector's Report,* (reports of site visits by CBM inspectors; these reports were succeeded by *Information Reports,* but their purposes were similar.)

Colorado Bureau of Mines, various dates, *Report to Bureau of Mines, State of Colorado* (annual report of mining activity made by mine owners.)

Colorado Department of Public Health & Environment and U.S. Environmental Protection Agency Region 8, 2014, *Update Fact Sheet Central City/Clear Creek Superfund Site* (https://semspub.epa.gov/work/08/1272343.pdf.)

Colorado Department of Public Health & Environment and U.S. Environmental Protection Agency Region 8, 2017, *Fifth Five-Year Review Report for Central City/ Clear Creek Superfund Site, Gilpin and Clear Creek Counties, Colorado* (https://semspub.epa.gov/work/08/100002154.pdf.)

Colorado Transcript, various issues and dates, newspaper published at Golden, Colorado.

Copper Handbook, The: A manual of the copper industry of the world, various annual issues.

Cox, Terry, 1989, *Inside the Mountains: a history of mining around Central City, Colorado,* Pruett Publishing, Boulder, CO.

Dynamac Corporation under contract with the U.S. Environmental Protection Agency, 2007, *Remediation System Evaluation: Central City/Clear Creek Superfund Site Argo Tunnel Water Treatment Plant, Idaho Springs, Colorado,* EPA contract 68-C-02-092.

Elk Mountain Pilot, various issues and dates, newspaper published at Crested Butte, Colorado.

Engineering and Mining Journal, The, various dates, weekly technical journal.

Environmental Protection Agency (Region VIII) and Colorado Department of Health and Environment, 2016, *Remedial Action Completion Report, Central City Clear Creek Superfund Site, Operable Unit 3, Argo Tunnel Flow-Control Bulkhead Project.*

Goodwin's Weekly, various issues and dates, newspaper published at Salt Lake City, Utah.

Harrison, J.E. and J. D. Wells, 1954, *Geology and Ore Deposits of the Freeland-Lamartine District, Clear Creek County, Colorado*, United States Geological Survey Trace Elements Investigations Report 295.

Harrison, J.E. and J. D. Wells, 1956, *Geology and Ore Deposits of the Freeland-Lamartine District, Clear Creek County, Colorado*, United States Geological Survey Bulletin 1032 B.

Harrison, J.E. and J. D. Wells, 1959, *Geology and Ore Deposits of the Chicago Creek Area, Clear Creek County, Colorado*, United States Geological Professional Paper 319.

Henderson, Charles W., 1926, *Mining in Colorado: A history of discovery, development and production*, United States Geological Survey Professional Paper 138.

Historic Utah, Inc., 1978, *National Register Nomination Form for Exchange Place Historic District.*

History Colorado, *Colorado Historic Newspapers Collection*, (www.coloradohistoricnewspapers.org), accessed 2019.

Hitzrot, H. W. and G. M. Meisel, 1985, in *SME Mineral Processing Handbook*, Society of Mining Engineers of the American Institute of Mining, Metallurgical and Petroleum Engineers.

Hollister, Ovando J., 1867, *The Mines of Colorado.*

Idaho Springs News, various issues and dates, newspaper published at Idaho Springs, Colorado.

Isern, Thomas Dean, 1974, *The Making of a Gold Rush: Pike's Peak, 1858-1860*, Oklahoma State University Master's thesis.

J. Willard Marriott Library, *Utah Digital Newspapers* (digitalnewspapers.org), accessed 2019, University of Utah at Salt Lake City.

Johnson, H. C., M.D., 1887, *The Historical Record: The early history of Wyoming Valley and contiguous territory*, vol 1, pg 55.

Kachejian, Brian, 2018, *History of New York's Fascination with the Flatiron Building*, www.ClassicNewYorkHistory.com.

Kross, Herman E. (ed.), 1983, *Documentary History of Banking and Currency in the United States*, four volumes.

Leadville Daily Chronicle, various issues and dates, newspaper published at Leadville, Colorado.

Leadville Daily Herald, various issues and dates, newspaper published at Leadville, Colorado.

Leadville Evening Chronicle, various issues and dates, newspaper published at Leadville, Colorado.

Leadville Herald Democrat, various issues and dates, newspaper published at Leadville, Colorado.

Leadville Weekly Herald, various issues and dates, newspaper published at Leadville, Colorado.

Los Angeles, County of, Registrar, County Clerk, 2019, *State of California Certification of Vital Record for Ida Hiram Newhouse.*

Luzerne Legal Register, The, various dates, Scranton, Pennsylvania.

Maxwell, James, 1977, *National Register Nomination Form for Argo Tunnel and Mill.*

Mines and Minerals, various dates, monthly journal dedicated to mining intelligence.

Mines Handbook, The: Succeeding the Copper Handbook, various annual issues.

Mining & Engineering World, various dates, bi-monthly journal dedicated to mining intelligence and methods.

Mining Investor, The, various dates, weekly journal dedicated to mining intelligence

Mining and Scientific Press, various dates, weekly journal dedicated to mining intelligence and methods.

Moench Robert H. and Alvery Ala Drake, Jr., 1966, *Economic Geology of the Idaho Springs District, Clear Creek and Gilpin Counties*, Colorado, United States Geological Survey Bulletin 1208.
Moench Robert H. and Alvery Ala Drake, Jr., 1966, *Mines and Prospects, Idaho Springs District, Clear Creek and Gilpin Counties, Colorado*, United States Geological Survey Open File Report 66-87.
Moody Publishing Company, various years, *Moody's Manual of Corporation Securities*.
National Cyclopaedia of American Biography, 1896, vol VI, James T. White and Company, publisher.
Newhouse, Samuel, Ancel Newhouse and Charles C. Parsons, Jan. 27, 1893, *Incorporation papers for the Argo Mining, Drainage, Transportation and Tunnel Company*.
Newhouse Tunnel Company, Ltd,. Apr. 19, 1893, *Articles of Association of the Newhouse Tunnel Company, Limited*.
Oliszewski, Alexander M, 1977, *Argo Tunnel and Mill, National Register of Historic Places Inventory Nomination Form*, National Park Service.
Powell, Allan Kent, 1994, Samuel Newhouse biography in *Utah History Encyclopedia*, University of Utah Press.
Queen Bee, various dates, newspaper published at Denver.
Quarterly Journal of Economics, February, 1916.
Real Estate Record and Builders' Guide, various dates, weekly record and intelligence of real estate transactions in New York, New York.
Rickard, Thomas A, 1917, *Flotation*, Mining & Scientific Press.
Rocky Mountain News, various dates, daily newspaper published at Denver, Colorado.
Salt Lake Herald Republican, various dates, published daily at Salt Lake City, Utah.
Salt Lake Mining Review, various dates, published weekly at Salt Lake City, Utah.
Salt Lake Telegram, various dates, published daily at Salt Lake City, Utah.
Salt Lake Tribune, various dates, published daily at Salt Lake City, Utah.
Sanborn Map Company, 1890, *Sanborn Fire Insurance Maps, from New York, Bronx, Manhattan, New York*, from Library of Congress, Sanborn Fire Insurance Maps Online Collection.
Sims, P. K. and others, 1963, *Geology of Uranium and Associated Ore Deposits Central Part of the Front Range Mineral Belt*, United States Geological Survey Professional Paper 371.
Smiley, Jerome C, 1901, *History of Denver*.
Solid Muldoon, The, various issues and dates, weekly newspaper published at Ouray, Colorado.
Sowell, Merle, 1976, *Historical Highlights of Idaho Springs: Mining camp days*.
Spurr, Josiah E. and George H. Garrey, 1908, *Economic Geology of the Georgetown Quadrangle (Together with the Empire District), Colorado*, United States Geological Survey Professional Paper 63.
Stewart, Kathleen C. and R. C. Severson, editors, 1994, *Guidebook on the Geology, History and Surface-Water Contamination and Remediation in the Area from Denver to Idaho Springs, Colorado*, United States Geological Survey, Circular 1097.
Temple Israel Foundation, www.JewishLeadville.org, *Biography of Samuel Newhouse*, accessed 2019, Leadville, Colorado.
United States Surveyor General, 1893, *Plat of the Claim of The Argo Mining, Drainage, Transportation and Tunnel Company, Mineral Survey No. 8580 A & B*.
United States Geological Survey, various dates, *Mineral Resources of the United States, Part I Metals*, annual statistics of metal recovery.
United States Geological Survey, 1922, *Guidebook of the Western United States*, Bulletin 707.
United States Department of State, various dates, *United States Passport Applications 1795-1925*, accessed via Ancestry.com.
United States Department of State, various dates, *Reports of Deaths of American Citizens Abroad, 1835-1975*, accessed via Ancestry.com.
various editors, 1896, *National Cyclopaedia of American Biography, volume IV*, James T. White & Co.

Warrum, Noble, ed., 1919, *Utah Since Statehood: Historical and Biographical, Vol. III.*
Wentz, Dennis A., 1877, *Quantity and Quality of Drainage from the Argo Tunnel and Other Sources Related to Metal Mining in Gilpin, Clear Creek and Park Counties, Colorado,* United States Geological Survey Open File Report 77-734.

Key to Abbreviations

ArgoPR	Argo Reduction and Ore Purchasing Company ore purchases
B707	USGS Bulletin 707
BDC	Boulder Daily Camera
CBMar	*Colorado Bureau of Mines Annual Report*
CBMir	*Colorado Bureau of Mines Inspector's Report*
CBMor	*Colorado Bureau of Mines, Report to Bureau of Mines*
CGE	*George Collins Papers*
CHbk	*The Copper Handbook*
COT	*Colorado Transcript*
CSM	Colorado School of Mines
Cox	Cox, *Inside the Mountains*
E&MJ	*Engineering & Mining Journal*
EMP	*Elk Mountain Pilot*
EPA	Environmental Protection Agency, Argo Tunnel bulkhead project
GW	*Goodwin's Weekly*
ISN	*Idaho Spring News*
LCC	*Carbonate Chronicle*
LDC	*Leadville Daily Chronicle*
LDH	*Leadville Daily Herald*
LEC	*Leadville Evening Chronicle*
LHD	*Leadville Herald Democrat*
LWH	*Leadville Weekly Herald*
LLR	*Luzerne Legal Register*
M&M	*Mines and Minerals*
M&EW	*Mining & Engineering World*
M&SP	*Mining & Scientific Press*
MHbk	*The Mines Handbook*
MinRes	*Mineral Resources of the United States*
Moody	*Moody's Manual of Corporation Securities*
NCAB	*National Cyclopaedia of American Biography*
PP94	Bastin and Hill, USGS Professional Paper 94
PP138	Henderson, USGS Professional Paper 138
QJE	*Quarterly Journal of Economics*
RDACA	*Reports of Deaths of American Citizens Abroad, 1835-1975*
RER	*Real Estate Record and Builders' Guide*
RMN	*Rocky Mountain News*
SLHR	*Salt Lake Herald-Republican*
SLMR	*Salt Lake Mining Review*
SLT	*Salt Lake Tribune*
SLTG	*Salt Lake Telegram*

TIF	*Temple Israel Foundation*
THR	*The Historical Record: The early history of Wyoming Valley*
TMI	*The Mining Investor*
USSG	United States Surveyor General plat
USPA	*United States Passport Applications, 1795-1925*
USS	*Utah Since Statehood*

The technical journals and references cited are all available on the web, primarily from HathiTrust.org or Books.Google.com.

Books dated prior to 1927 can usually be found on the web at the two aforementioned sites as well as at JSTOR.org. Books dated after 1927 often need to be viewed at larger libraries or borrowed through the Interlibrary Loan system. Some can be purchased from specialty booksellers on the web, especially general interest titles dated from the 1970s onward.

Geologic references can be downloaded in their entireties from the web site of the United States Geological Survey.

Sanborn Fire Insurance maps were consulted for locations of historic features in Idaho Springs, Nevadaville, Central City, and Black Hawk. Complete collections are viewable at the Library of Congress website.

Researching historic newspapers is a hit and miss endeavor. Complete runs are rarely available. Newspapers are best found on the web by searching for place or state names combined with the words, "historic newspapers." Search results depend on the accuracy of transcriptions and most newspapers were transcribed by optical character recognition. Transcriptions can be absolutely horrible. Colorado's are dramatically better than most.

Federal publications, like those from the EPA, are best found on the web by searching for titles directly.

Official vital records are best found by contacting states or counties where births, marriages, and deaths may have occurred. Many locations have public-facing interfaces through third-party vendors. Genealogical resources such as Ancestry.org, FamilySearch.org, and FindAGrave.com are excellent places to start.

Don't be afraid to call any library directly and ask for help. Many can be contacted by online chats. I have yet to encounter a research librarian who was not maximally helpful.

Endnotes

1. PP138, pg 5
2. Hollister, pg 76
3. Hollister, pg 68
4. PP138, 1926, pg 88
5. M&M, Aug., 1900, pp 31-33
6. PP94, Plate IV
7. TMI, Feb. 27, 1911, pg 44
8. M&M, Aug., 1900, pp 31-33
9. USSG
10. Argo Tunnel incorporation papers
11. Newhouse Tunnel Co incorporation papers
12. ISN, Oct. 20, 1893
13. ISN, Oct. 13, 1893 and M&M, Aug., 1906, pg 36
14. *Queen Bee* newspaper (Denver), Dec. 20, 1893
15. M&M, Aug., 1906, pg 37
16. ISN, Jul. 26, 1895
17. TMI, Mar. 29, 1909, pg 147
18. ISN, Jul. 26, 1895
19. Maxwell, James, 1977
20. CHbk, 1905 issue for 1904, pg 198
21. M&M, Aug., 1906, pg 37
22. M&M, Sep., 1906, pg 74
23. *Daily Journal* (Telluride), Mar. 17, 1905
24. E&MJ, Aug. 26, 1905
25. Music and lyrics by Theodore Metz and Joe Hayden, 1895
26. PP94, pg 306
27. *Eagle County Blade*, Feb. 21, 1907
28. TMI, May 25, 1908, pg 42c
29. TMI, Jul. 6, 1908, pg 193
30. CHbk, 1911 issue for 1910
31. TMI, Mar. 29, 1909, pg 147
32. TMI, Jul. 4, 1910, pg 197
33. TMI, May 28, 1910, pg 141
34. TMI, Jul. 11, 1910, pg 244
35. TMI, Feb. 27, 1911, pg 37
36. TMI, Oct. 24, 1910, pg 297
37. TMI, Fe. 217, 1911, pg 44
38. MHbk, 1922 issue for 1921, pg 602
39. EMP, Jul. 18, 1912
40. ArgoPR, 1914-1918
41. ArgoPR, 1914-1918
42. MHbk, 1922 issue for 1921, pg 600
43. SLMR, Feb. 28, 1921
44. COT, Mat. 17, 1921
45. CBMir, Jul. 9, 1926
46. CBMir, Jul. 29, 1924
47. CBMir, Jul. 7, 1931
48. CGE, purchased for $175,000
49. CGE, purchased Jan. 27, 1937
50. CSM, undated map north end of Argo Tunnel
51. Cox, pg 37
52. CBMor, Mar. 17, 1944; this report suggested that flood waters probably came from mine workings connected to the Ophir-Burroughs shaft.
53. RMN, Jan. 20-21, 1943, names of "Albert" confirmed by headstone in Idaho Springs Cemetery; "Mettras" by Draft Registration Card; "Lewis" by .CBMar, 1943.
54. CBMir, Oct. 25, 1954
55. CBMor, Jan. 1, 1955
56. CBMir, Mar. 1, 1955
57. EPA, bulkhead completion report, 2016
58. *Ogden Daily Standard*, Jan. 7, 1902
59. *Summit County Journal*, Nov. 11, 1905
60. *Montrose Daily Press*, Aug. 24, 1910
61. *Republican-Advocate* (Sterling), Aug. 31, 1910
62. M&SP, Nov. 28, 1914, pg 833.
63. M&SP, Nov. 28, 1914, pg 836
64. CBMar, 1914, pg 87
65. CBMar, 1914, pg 89
66. E&MJ, Jul. 4, 1914, pg 2
67. E&MJ, Jul. 4, 1914, pg 1
68. E&MJ, Aug., 1, 1914, pg 217
69. E&MJ, Jul. 4, 1914, pg 1
70. CBMir, Dec. 29, 1915
71. E&MW, Feb. 12, 1916, pg 372
72. Rickard, T. A., 1917
73. EMP, Apr. 17, 1919
74. E&MJ, Nov. 3, 1920, pg 960 and 968
75. M&SP, Nov. 16, 1912, pg 639
76. E&MJ, Aug. 1, 1914, pg 217
77. E&MJ. Nov. 28, 1914, pg 837
78. MinRes, 1916, pg 352
79. M&SP, Mar. 25, 1916
80. CHbk, 1914 issue for 1913
81. USS, pg 733
82. USPA, Samuel Newhouse, 1921 and 1923
83. United States census, 1860, estimates based on birth of Mott in 1858
84. United States census, 1860
85. United States census, 1870
86. NCAB, pg 402
87. LLR, Dec. 12, 1873
88. Quoted in LLR, Jan. 12, 1877
89. THR, pg 55, also *Record of the Times* (Wilkes-Barre, PA), Apr. 21, 1879
90. TIF

[91] *Record of the Times* (Wilkes-Barre, PA), Oct. 20, 1883
[92] LDH, Nov. 13, 1881
[93] COT, Jul. 18, 1900
[94] LDH, Jul. 1, 1882
[95] LDH and LDC, advertisements in numerous issues
[96] Death certificate of Ida Hiram Stingley Newhouse, Mar. 17, 1955, Los Angles County, California, *Certification of Vital Record*
[97] United States census, 1870
[98] United States census, 1880
[99] LDH, Dec. 17, 1882
[100] LDH, Jan. 4, 1883
[101] LWH, Mar. 31, 1881
[102] LHD, Sep. 4, 1886
[103] Smiley, 1901, *History of Denver*
[104] The Successful American, Aug., 1900, pg 22
[105] *The Solid Muldoon*, Jun., 25, 1886
[106] USS, pg 733
[107] THR, pg 55
[108] Ballenger and Richards, 1889
[109] Holabird Western Americana, *Fall Americana Auction*, Oct., 2019, lot 3356, stock certificate with Loveland and Newhouse signatures.
[110] Colorado incorporation records
[111] *London Evening Standard*, Dec. 2, 1895 and *Investors' Guardian* (London), Nov. 15, 1890
[112] COT, Jul. 11, 1890, also known as Tyndale mine
[113] USSG
[114] *Aspen Weekly Times*, Jan. 9, 1892
[115] Incorporation papers for the Argo Mining, Drainage, Transportation and Tunnel Company, Jan. 27, 1893
[116] Articles of Association of the Newhouse Tunnel Company, Limited, Apr. 19, 1893
[117] BDC, Mar. 29, 1894
[118] *Colorado Daily Chieftain* (Pueblo), Mar. 2, 1895
[119] BDC, Oct. 17, 1896
[120] LDH, Apr. 16, 1884
[121] LDH, May 27, 1884
[122] LCC, Oct. 25, 1884
[123] LEC, Nov. 30, 1888
[124] SLT, Sep. 22, 1894
[125] SLHR, Jul. 15, 1895
[126] SLT, Oct. 4, 1896
[127] Moody, 1904 and CHbk, 1902
[128] SLT, Apr. 22, 1899
[129] SLTG, Oct. 4, 1896
[130] CHbk
[131] QJE, pp 387-407 by F. Earnest Richter
[132] SLHR, Feb. 21, 1899
[133] SLT, Apr. 13, 1898
[134] CHbk, 1905
[135] SLT, Jun. 3, 1898
[136] Moody, 1904
[137] B707, pg 237
[138] SLT, Apr. 22, 1899
[139] SLT, Jun. 14, 1899
[140] M&M, Jul., 1900
[141] *Fairplay Plume*, May 11, 1900
[142] *Brooklyn Daily Eagle*, Mar. 11, 1900
[143] RER, May 6, 1899, pg 817
[144] RER, Mar. 2, 1901, pg 817
[145] RER, May 6, 1899, pg 817
[146] RER, Feb. 9, 1901, pg 285
[147] RER, Mar. 2, 1901, pg 357
[148] RER, Jan. 1, 1902, pg 11
[149] RER, Jul. 20, 1901, pg 75
[150] Warburg Realty, website WarburgRealty.com
[151] CHbk, 1905 for 1904
[152] CHbk, 1911; organized New York, February 28, 1910;
[153] SLT, Apr. 15, 1904
[154] SLT, Apr. 17, 1904
[155] Historic Utah, Inc.
[156] SLHR, Apr. 4, 1908
[157] GW, Jan. 7, 1914
[158] SLT, Aug. 28, 1907
[159] GW, Feb. 14, 1914
[160] SLT, Mar. 28, 1915
[161] SLHR, Mar. 3, 1915
[162] GW, Dec. 7, 1918
[163] SLT, Feb. 11, 1917
[164] *The Mining American*, Sep. 29, 1917. pg 22
[165] SLTG, Mar. 15, 1916
[166] *The Hotel World*, Oct. 18, 1919
[167] SLMR, Jul. 5, 1923
[168] SLMR, Jul. 30, 1923
[169] SLMR, Nov. 30, 1923
[170] SLTG, Feb. 6, 1924
[171] SLTG, Spr. 30, 1924
[172] SLMR, May 15, 1924
[173] SLMR, Jul. 30, 1924
[174] also SLTG, Nov. 28, 1924
[175] RDACA, Oct. 16, 1930
[176] USPA, Ida Newhouse, Feb. 3, 1925, SLTG Mar. 4, 1925
[177] RDACA, Oct. 16, 1930
[178] State of California Certification of Vital Record for Ida Hiram Newhouse

INDEX

All named mines, shafts and veins are grouped under the headings, "Mines and veins."

amalgamation, 4, 13, 63, 66-67
Americus Mine disaster, 46
Arapahoe City, 9
Argo claims, 19
Argo Mill, business structure, 59-61
Argo Tipple, 37
Argo Tunnel bulkhead, 50–51
Argo water treatment plant, 50–51
Aspen silver district, 50
Auraria, 9
Black Hawk, 6, 11, 12, 16, 18
blasting patterns, 28-29
Boston Building, 106, 111
British investment in Newhouse projects, 19, 21, 24, 32, 36
Cherry Creek, 9
Chicago Creek, 10, 50
Clear Creek, 10, 11
   North Clear Creek, 10, 11
   South Clear Creek, 10, 19
Clear Creek County mines (general), 12-13, 44, 50, 89
Colorado Territory, 50
Companies
   Amalgamated Copper Co., 95-96
   American Smelting & Refining Co. (ASARCO), 80
   Anaconda Copper Mining Co., 95, 107
   Argo Mining and Tunnel Company, 36
   Argo Mining, Drainage, Transportation & Tunnel Co., 19-21, 45
   Argo Reduction and Ore Purchasing Co., 56, 83
   Argo Transportation & Tunnel Co., Ltd., 32
   Argo Tunnel & Mining Co., Ltd., 24, 26
   Bingham Central Mining Co., 105
   Bingham Mines Co., 105
   Bingham Standard Copper Co., 105
   Boston Consolidated Copper & Gold Mining Co., Ltd., 97, 105
   Boston Consolidated Mining Co., 97, 98, 100, 105
   Burroughs Pool Mining Co., 44
   Butte Copper Exploration Co., 105
   California-Hidden Treasure Mines Co., 44
   California & Colorado Consolidated Tunnel & Mining Co., 87, 89
   Casper-Embar Petroleum Co., 111
   Chain O' Mines, Inc., 44
   Colorado Central Railroad Co., 16
   Colorado Gold Corp., 44
   Colorado & Southern RR Co., 16, 37
   Cumberland Realty Co., 100-101
   Denver Coal Co., 89, 109
   Denver & Intermountain Railway Co., 103, 105
   Denver, Lakewood & Golden Railroad Co., 89-90, 98-99, 103, 109
   Dominion Copper Co., 105
   Environmental Protection Agency, 48-49
   Galli Mining Co., 44
   Gauntlet Gold Mining Co., 35, 39
   Gem Mining Co., 43-44
   Gem Tunnel Co., 44
   Gilpin-Eureka Mines Co., 41
   Gilpin-Eureka Mining & Milling Co, 41
   Gilpin County Chamber of Commerce, 35-36
   Gilpin Railroad Co., 116
   Gilpin Tramway Co., 14, 16, 116
   Grand Gulch Copper Mining Co., 105
   Gunnell Mining & Milling Co., 38
   Highland Boy Gold Mining Co., 94-95
   Hot Time Transportation Drainage & Tunnel Co., 33
   Idaho Gold Corp., 112
   Kelsey Enterprises, 47

King Kong Mines, 44
Louisiana Consolidated Gold Mining Co., 105
Magma Superior Copper Co., 111
Majestic Copper Co., 105
Montana Boy Consolidated Mines Co., 105
Montana Revenue Gold Mining Co., 105
Montgomery Mountain Mining Co., 105
Newhouse Mines & Smelters Co., 102-103
Newhouse Tunnel Co., Ltd, 19, 21, 24
Newhouse Transfer Co., 66-67
Nipissing Mining Co., 105
Ohio Kentucky Mining Co., 105
Old Town Consolidated Mining Co., 32
Quartz Hill Mining Co., 44
Silver King Consolidated Mining Co., 105
Standard Oil Trust, 95-96
Tremont Mining Co., 42
Union Carbonate Mines, Inc, 44
Utah Consolidated Gold Mines, Ltd., 94-96
Utah Consolidated Mining Co., 96
Western Nevada Copper Co., 105
Walker Mining Co., 107
Comstock Lode, 17
concentration table, 67, 69, 71, 73-74
cone classifier, 70
Cripple Creek gold district, 50
crushing, 61-63
custom mill, definition, 53
cyanidation, 67, 69, 74-75
Denver, 16, 19, 44
Denver City, 9
Depressions, recessions, 41, 42, 43, 80, 109, 115, 116
Door classifier, 67,69, 70, 71
electric locomotive haulage, 27, 43
Empire, 56, 73, 115
fatalities, 52
Flatiron Building, 99, 101-102, 105-106
Fort Laramie, 9
Forty-niners, 9
froth flotation, 71, 75-77
Fuller Building, 100-102
Georgetown, 56, 76, 89, 115, 116
Gilpin County Chamber of Commerce, 35-36

Gilpin County mines (general), 8, 12-13, 44, 50, 89, 116
gold panning, 4 , 9, 10, 11, 18, 72
gold prices, 12, 26, 42, 43, 53, 58, 59, 81
gold prices through time, 77
gold prices, increase to $35, 77, 81, 116
Gold Rush, 1858, 9
Gold Rush, 1859, 9-11
gold telluride, 50
gold veins, 15
Golden, 49, 81, 91, 115
gravity separation, 72-73
Gregory Diggings, 6, 11
hoisting, 13-14, 20
Idaho Springs, 10, 12, 16, 18, 19
Idahoe, 10
Jackson's Diggings, 6, 10
Jackson Monument, 10
Jason and the Golden Fleece, 73
Kansas Mine disaster, 34, 46–48
Kansas Territory, 9
Lake County, 50
Leadville, 85
Leadville silver district, 50
lode gold, 18
Marnes la Coquette , 111, 112, 113
Marnes, château de, 111, 112, 113
mechanical drills, 20, 21, 31
mercury, 13, 63, 66-67, 74
Mines and veins
  Aduddell, 16, 19, 25, 30, 33, 34, 41
  Aduddell Lateral, 34
  Americus, 46, 116
  Anaconda, 95, 107
  A.Y., 93
  Belman, 25, 33
  Big Five Tunnel, 49
  Bingham Canyon, 38
  Burroughs, 39
  Cactus, 102-103, 106, 107
  Calhoun, 25,32, 41
  Calhoun Lateral, 34
  California, 19, 25, 32, 45
  Compeer, 32
  Compensation, 32
  Concrete, 18, 19, 25, 34, 38, 41
  Druid, 30
  Dyke, 25, 32
  Dyke vein Lateral, 34
  Edgardine, 33

El Socorro, 112
Eureka, 18, 19, 22-23, 34, 38, 41
Fisk, 46
Freighter's Friend, 25, 34
Frontenac, 16, 19, 25, 34
Gem, 19, 24, 25, 26, 33, 34, 39, 41, 43, 44
Gem Lateral, 43
Gilpin-Eureka, 41
Golden Treasure, 45
Grand Army, 18, 25, 38, 41
Granite Mountain, 93
Great Mammoth, 35
Gregory, 35
Gunnell, 18, 25, 34, 38, 39-41, 44
Half & Half, 33
Hayes & Wheeler, 25, 35
Hidden Treasure, 45
Highland Boy, 38
Hot Time Lateral, 34, 32-35, 39
Hubert, 25, 45
Illinois, 25, 32
Japan, 32
Kansas, 17, 25, 39, 45, 46–48, 52
Kansas Lateral, 34
Kennedy, 94
Lucky Boy, 105
Mammoth, 35
Mammoth lateral, 33, 34, 35, 39
Minnie, 93
Morning Star, 30, 33
North Gunnell, 32
North Hubert, 45
Old Town, 25, 32, 34, 41
Ophir-Burroughs, 25, 32, 34
Ophir-Burroughs Lateral, 34
Pozo, 25
Prize, 25, 32, 34, 41, 45
Prussian, 91
Queen, 33
Revenue, 93, 95
Saratoga, 19, 24, 30, 31, 32, 34
Saratoga Lateral, 34, 39
Seaton, 25, 33
Slaughterhouse, 45
Sleepy Hollow, 116
South Gunnell, 32
Stanley, 19
Sun & Moon, 19, 25, 26, 33, 34, 41
Sun & Moon Lateral, 34, 39
Sutro Tunnel, 17

Tindale, 90
Tropic, 23, 25, 33
Ulay, 93
Ute, 93
Wellington, 30, 32
William Penn, 26
mule haulage, 26-27
Nebraska Territory, 9
Nevadaville, 6, 11, 16, 19, 45
Newhouse Building, 106, 111
Newhouse Hotel, 106, 107, 108, 110
Newhouse, Utah, 102, 103
ore, definition, 26
Ouray, 85
Pikes Peak Gold Rush, 9
Pitkin County, 50
placer, placer gold, 4, 11, 18, 55, 57, 115
Prosser Gulch, 18
rake classifier, 70
reduction mill definition, 58
Russell Gulch, 11, 12, 19, 32
Sacramento City, 10
Scranton, PA, 85
shaker table, 67, 69, 71, 73-74
Silverton, 19
Smelters
  ASARCO, 80, 116
  Boston & Colorado, 12, 115, 116
  Modern, 80
smelting, 4, 54-55
South Platte River, 9, 11
Spitzkasten, 67, 70
stamp mill, 61-63, 67, 68, 69, 71
Superfund law, 48
Superfund site, 49
Teller County, 50
U.S. Mint, 57, 67, 68, 69
Vasquez Fork, see Clear Creek
vein gold, 11, 15
water problems and drainage, ,13-14, 16,
  18, 20, 23, 27, 30, 36, 41, 46, 47
Wilfley table, 67, 69, 71, 73-74
World War I, 16, 42, 46, 59, 71, 75, 76,
  80, 109, 110-111, 115

www.ingramcontent.com/pod-product-compliance
Lightning Source LLC
Chambersburg PA
CBHW031430290426
44110CB00011B/609